VISIONS

BY DAVID P. DOUGHTY

Joy Publishing
P.O. Box 9901
Fountain Valley, CA 92708

And afterward, I will pour out my Spirit on all people. Your sons and daughters will prophesy, your old men will dream dreams, your young men will see visions. Even on my servants, both men and women, I will pour out my Spirit in those days. I will show wonders in the heavens and on the earth, blood and fire and billows of smoke. The sun will be turned to darkness and the moon to blood before the coming of the great and dreadful day of the LORD. And everyone who calls on the name of the LORD will be saved.

Joel 2:28 - 32 (NIV)

VISIONS

by

DAVID P. DOUGHTY

Published by:
Joy Publishing
P.O. Box 9901
Fountain Valley, 92708

Printed in the United States of America

ISBN 0-939513-27-7

Cover designed by Dennis McLain
Text design by Tricia Young

FOREWORD

Albert Camus once said, "I shall tell you a secret, my friend. Do not wait for the Last Judgment. It takes place every day." Indeed, the Living Spirit of Christ is with you at this moment, and it is by no mistake that you are holding this book in your hands. You have been given this gift because God has sent it to you. I pray that you will read all of it with an open heart.

As a word of encouragement, I would say something about the writer. David has been a friend of mine since our college days at Louisiana Tech in the early 1980s. He is the "All-American Guy." He is intelligent, polished, successful, and he has the respect of all who know him. The point I am making is that he is an example of stability and consistency. He is not coming from "left field." I have the utmost trust in his integrity, and I fully believe the validity of the experience he will share with you in these pages.

John W. Gardner once said, "To sensible men, every day is a day of reckoning." God has already used David's account to change many lives. The next one can be yours! Please read on.

Grace and peace,
Marcus Murphy, Pastor
First Baptist Church
Delhi, Louisiana

INTRODUCTION

Who can be believed? Who can be trusted to tell the truth?

These are important questions, especially in my line of work. I'm an attorney, now in my eighth year of private practice, a partner of the Cotton Bolton Hoychick & Doughty law firm in Rayville, Louisiana. I am also an assistant District Attorney for the Fifth Judicial District. In order to establish the credibility of a witness, I will present that person's background and credentials, and let the judge or jury hear his voice, and observe him telling his story. In reading this book, you won't be able to look me in the eye to determine if I'm telling the truth. But I hope you can hear my voice as you read and believe. This is a journal of remarkable, incredible events, and I only ask you to keep an open mind.

I'm not a fanatic, nor do I have any formal religious education. I'm a practical, both-feet-on-the-ground type of guy. I have a beautiful wife, two kids, a dog, and a mortgage. I graduated summa cum laude from both Louisiana Tech University and Tulane Law School. As my brother Terry has told me, "You are the least likely person I know to experience this. Maybe that's why the dreams were given to you. If it were someone else, I'd think they were crazy."

Well, you may still think I'm crazy. But maybe, just maybe, you'll see that God is doing something remarkable in the world today and that soon, something spectacular is going to happen. Very soon.

David Doughty
Rayville, Louisiana
August 1997

TABLE OF CONTENTS

Chapter 1 **THE DREAM** 1

Chapter 2 **EXPERIENCING GOD** 4

Chapter 3 **THE SECOND DREAM** 15

Chapter 4 **PROMISE KEEPERS** 17

Chapter 5 **TWELVE WEEKS** 21

Chapter 6 **THE LAST WEEK** 30

Chapter 7 **THE THIRD DREAM** 43

Chapter 8 **I AM NOT ALONE** 51

Chapter 9 **THE DREAMS CONTINUE** 55

Chapter 10 **THE LAST TIME** 58

Chapter 11 **REVELATIONS** 62

Chapter 12 **SPIRITUAL WARFARE** 67

Chapter 13 **THE WIND BLOWS** 75

Chapter 14 **RIPPLE EFFECTS** 80

Chapter 15 **TWO MINUTE WARNING** 90

Chapter 16 **ALL IN THE FAMILY** 96

Chapter 17 **SIGNS, SIGNS, EVERYWHERE A SIGN** ... 102

Chapter 18 **IN THIS SIGN, CONQUER** 112

EPILOGUE 117

Chapter 1

THE DREAM

Life can change in the blink of an eye. On December 20, 1995, I learned that firsthand. That night I went to sleep, and things have never been the same.

The dream began in a very ordinary way. I was standing outside my home in the front yard, raking leaves near a tall magnolia tree. The sky was overcast, and it seemed to be in the fall or winter of the year. Suddenly, a red cloud appeared like a pillar out of the sky. It was positioned behind a circular grove of trees in a vacant field across the street. Thousands of lights glowed inside the reddish cloud, moving upward like a swarm of fireflies. As I looked closer, the lights took on the form of people. It wasn't fireflies. People were rising up into the clouds!

"Oh, my God! Jesus is coming," I thought aloud. This may not have been the proper thing to say or think, but nevertheless, it's what I said. As soon as I said these words, I was lifted toward the sky. The clouds parted and the heavens seemed to open up above me — it was like something out of a Stephen Spielberg movie. Instantly I was brought into the brightest white light I've ever seen. Pure light. Pure joy. It was the greatest feeling I've experienced.

Just as quickly, I was awake, my heart pounding in my chest as if it were going to explode. I was "electrified"— every nerve was tingling with excitement. I could barely catch my breath. What in the world had just happened to me?

As I lay in bed with my wife Suzette asleep beside me, a myriad of emotions flooded my senses. Joy at what I had experienced. Anger that it had not been real. The experience was so vivid it was hard to believe that it was only a dream. What struck me was the suddenness of how quickly it had happened. I was just raking leaves. Then the red cloud, the white light and the absolutely incredible feeling of love and peace. Besides joy and anger, I also felt fear. What did this mean? What was God saying to me? Was I supposed to become some type of modern-day prophet? I didn't want to be a prophet. I liked my life and didn't want it to change. Then I became afraid. Was I going crazy? Had this **really** just happened to me?

These thoughts raced through my head, a Bible verse popped into my mind:

> But the angel said to them, "Do not be afraid. I bring you good news of great joy that will be for all the people." Luke 2:10 (NIV)

Why this verse came to mind, I don't know. Maybe it was because Christmas was just around the corner. However, there was no angel or Charlton Heston-like voice to explain the dream to me. It was about 3:00 a.m. when I awoke. Needless to say, I didn't sleep much the rest of the night.

The next morning I was still incredibly shaken by what I had experienced. The entire experience seemed surreal. I went to my law office early that morning trying to figure it out. When my law partners Johnny Hoychick and Terry Doughty (my brother) arrived, I spoke with them about it at length. Both could see how disturbed I was. My hands were shaking. Me, an attorney who has been described at having ice water in my veins: The "Ice Man". I never get nervous, yet here I was, shaking like a child.

The questions boiled out of me. Was God speaking to me? If so, what was He saying? And what did He want me to do?

Of course, they couldn't answer this, but Johnny told me that I needed to let the Holy Spirit guide me. I had depositions scheduled that morning in Jonesville, Louisiana. The trip goes through a hilly, pine-filled area between Peck and Leland. As I drove that morning, the sky overhead was overcast, just as it had been in the dream. I couldn't get the vision out of my mind. What was going on?

As weeks passed, the initial shock began to diminish. I shared the experience with only a few people: my wife Suzette, my pastor Dr. Ernest Winburn, close friends such as Lamar Lane, Monty Hogg, and Tom Allen. But I didn't openly tell everyone. They'd probably think that I had gone crazy, or just pass it off to my vivid imagination. There's an old saying that "Time heals all wounds". I guess you could also say that time fades all memories. As the winter of 1996 rolled on, the intense joy, electricity, and confusion faded, but not the vividness of the experience. "Maybe it was just another dream," I told myself. But deep down inside I knew it wasn't.

Chapter 2

EXPERIENCING GOD

The spring came, and I took a discipleship course taught at our church called "Experiencing God: Knowing and Doing the Will of God" by Dr. Henry Blackaby and Claude V. King. The thirteen-week course was taught by Johnny Hoychick and Susan Clark, and focused on the Seven Realities of Experiencing God:

1. God is always at work around you.

2. God pursues a continuing love relationship with you that is real and personal.

3. God invites you to become involved with Him in His work.

4. God speaks by the Holy Spirit through the Bible, prayer, circumstances, and the church to reveal Himself, His purposes, and His ways.

5. God's invitation for you to work with Him always leads you to a crisis of belief that requires faith and action.

6. You must make major adjustments in your life to join God in what He is doing.

7. You come to know God by experiencing as you obey Him and He accomplishes His work through you.

Little did I know how vivid and real these "seven realities" would become to me. During this course, several important things happened in my spiritual growth, perhaps preparing me for what would come later.

1. Mr. Jimmy's cancer.

My father-in-law Jimmy Hopson was diagnosed with bladder cancer in the spring of 1996. "Mr. Jimmy" is like a second father to me. He loves me like his own son. He has two daughters Suzette and Stacey. I was probably the son he never had. That's true because Suzette and I were high school sweethearts, dating since the ages of sixteen and fifteen. I grew up in their household. Suzette and I were married after I had graduated from Louisiana Tech. Mr. Jimmy is also Chairman of the Board of Guaranty Bank and Mayor of the Town of Delhi.

Mrs. Sue Hopson called me at the office, her voice trembling.

"David, Jimmy has cancer." The words froze me. Mr. Jimmy was going into the hospital in Vicksburg. I could feel a terrible emptiness in the pit of my stomach. Suzette and I soon learned that he had a tumor the size of an orange in his bladder. The two of us walked into a small prayer room at the hospital, dropping down to our knees and pleading with God to heal him. The 23rd psalms came to mind. We were walking through the valley of the shadow of death. The tumor was removed from Mr. Jimmy's bladder and was found to be malignant. The doctors warned that his entire bladder might have to be removed if the cancer had grown into the muscle walls of the bladder. That would result in a colostomy, and Mr. Jimmy would have a "bag" the rest of his life. While we waited that weekend for the test results, Suzette and I were anxious, but we spent a lot of time in prayer. It's strange that often it takes adversity to awaken us spiritually. Most of the time we simply live our lives in a self-centered manner, caught up in our own little world, and it takes something extreme for God to get our attention. This was extreme. And believe me, He had our attention. Suzette was upset and couldn't find any peace over her father's condition. On Friday night of that weekend, we knelt at the foot of our bed and prayed that God would give her a peace about it, regardless of the test results. We also sought healing from God for her father.

The next day Suzette received a phone call from Leah Pardue, a friend from Mangham. She had heard about Mr. Jimmy's situation and shared with Suzette about her father's similar problems a few years ago. He had cancer of the bladder and a colostomy. The bag had not slowed her father down at all. This phone call came "out of the blue" and was just the thing Suzette needed. People often think they must hear some voice from heaven in order for God to speak to us. But in my experience He uses people, each one of us, to act. That day He used Leah Pardue to lift my wife's spirits. It couldn't have come at a better time.

The results came back, and Mr. Jimmy's bladder didn't have to be removed. It was the best of all possible results. He would still have to undergo chemotherapy, but it was a miracle for Mr. Jimmy and our family. And we had truly witnessed God at work.

2. Dr. Winburn's heart.

Dr. Ernest Winburn is the pastor at First Baptist Church in Rayville, the church I was born and raised in. He's been at our church for approximately ten years. I don't know a finer man. Like me, he loves sports. He's a down-to-earth man of God, humble and caring. I may have heard better preachers, but I've never known a better **pastor**. Although, he's in fine physical shape, Dr. Winburn has had some severe health problems recently, including a collapsed lung. During the spring of 1996, he learned that he had blockage in his arteries and was scheduled to undergo surgery on a Monday. The wives of some of our deacons suggested that we, as a deacon body, pray over Dr. Winburn and "lay hands" on him. It seems that most good suggestions in our church come from women. The real work of the church for years had been done by women, with a lot of the men simply not participating. Sunday night, before evening church, the deacons met in the "old church building" — a recent renovation of the original sanctuary. Each deacon went by Dr. Winburn, who was seated, and prayed over him, placing their hands on his body. For the first time since I was elected as a deacon in 1992, I felt that we were truly doing what God wanted us to do. Our deacon meetings were largely business oriented, managing a church budget of almost $400,000. But this was spiritual, something special.

As we prayed over Dr. Winburn that night, there were no flashes of lightning or supernatural fireworks. It was just a quiet, sincere, heartfelt time of prayer. The next day we found out that God had heard us. Dr. Winburn's doctors examined his heart again; this time finding no blockages. No clogged arteries, no surgery. No surgery, big miracle.

3. James' salvation.

My two children are the true joy in life. James is eight (second grade) and Caroline is five (nursery school). Caroline is a pistol and has the sweetest little smile on the planet. I guess every son wants to be like his father, and James is no different. He tells everyone that he looks just like his daddy except that his hair is "brownish-black" rather than black. Although is hair is only a medium brown, at best, James is convinced that it's getting darker. He also has an incredible persistence about him, sometimes driving his mother and me insane with his constant requests. Once he gets something in his mind, he doesn't easily let it go.

In the spring of 1996, James began asking Suzette and me questions about God, salvation and heaven. His heart was really being stirred. With James' intelligence, he wouldn't just ask me the easy questions.

"Daddy, did Judas have to betray Jesus?"

He definitely wasn't lobbing me "softball" questions.

James wanted to be baptized. Suzette and I talked with him about these things and I decided to speak to Dr. Winburn.

One Wednesday evening, James and I went to Dr. Winburn's office. He asked James some questions concerning his beliefs about Jesus and told him that to be saved he had to confess his sins, believe in Jesus and ask him into his heart.

James said a prayer:

"Dear God, I know that I've sinned and done some bad things. Give me a clean heart and make me a Christian boy. I love you. Amen."

Simple words, a childlike faith. That's what Jesus wants from all of us. Tears welled up in my eyes as I heard my son's prayer and felt the joy of knowing that God had just written his name in the Book of Life. We wouldn't just be spending our life on earth together, but all eternity.

4. Men's prayer group.

In the early 1990s, some young men in our church formed a prayer group at 6:00 a.m. on Wednesday mornings. The men's prayer group was initially a great success. One morning we were discussing prayer requests. An old high school friend of mine, Al Morris, was mentioned. I hadn't seen Al in more than five or six years. We thought he was living in Atlanta, but weren't sure. Most of his family had left Rayville and his father, a former District Judge, had passed away a few years before. We prayed about Al's relationship with God.

Later that same day, I was busy at work when my secretary announced over the phone intercom that someone wanted to see me.

"Al Morris is here to meet you, David."

"Al Morris?"

"Yes, Al Morris would like to talk to you. Says he's an old friend of yours."

I thought my heart was going to stop. Al Morris. The same one we had prayed for just that morning. I knew God answered prayers, but not this quick.

Al met me in my office. He had been traveling from Atlanta to Monroe, Louisiana (about thirty miles west of Rayville) where his mother lived. As he was nearing the Rayville exit on Interstate 20, he just felt like he needed to stop and see me. I told Al that we had prayed about him that same morning. We were both flabbergasted. He had been through some troubling times, but he did have a personal relationship with Jesus Christ. I didn't know if anyone would believe me that Al Morris had suddenly appeared out of nowhere, so I took him around to several of the other guys in our prayer group who also been high school friends of Al. They were as stunned and blessed by the incident as I was.

This men's prayer group lasted for awhile, but interest waned and it eventually just faded away. Unfortunately, that's what happens in most people's spiritual lives. There's a brief flame that burns bright, but then we smoulder out, going back to the rat race, the memories of God's work in our lives slipping into forgetfulness.

One of my close friends, Ricky Cooper, was also taking the Experiencing God class that spring of 1996. Ricky had experienced a dramatic change in his life, becoming one of the most "on fire" Christians I've ever seen. His excitement was contagious. He was the catalyst in the forming of a new men's prayer group. No, I take that back. The Holy Spirit was the catalyst. Ricky was the instrument, the person He worked through. We first met at 6:00 a.m. on Thursday morning at our law office annex building, seven of us: Ricky, Johnny Hoychick, Rayland Trisler, Wayne McManus, Bruce Parker, Dr. Ernest Winburn, and me. Later, we also had a powerful infusion from Joe Senn. Joe is a Rayville native, once renowned for his football skills and his ability to whip any man in the area. But God had different plans for this big linebacker of a man. Joe gave his life to Christ and was called into the ministry. Later, within the last few years, he was called to become a full-time evangelist. He is now the staff evangelist at First Baptist of Rayville, a church he grew up in. It's been said that a prophet is not without honor except in his homeland. That doesn't fit with Joe. The impact of seeing this once rowdy youth now a devout man of God has been enormous. Joe preaches and prays hard, loud, and full of the Holy Spirit. I can truly say that I didn't really know much about group prayer until I got into a session with Joe and company. As one person is voicing a prayer, several others lift up these prayers aloud in an almost hum of sound. Initially, I was uncomfortable in praying and affirming another prayer out loud, but practice made me more at ease with it.

At some of our first prayer sessions, I prayed for my father and mother. My parents were together during my youth, but were divorced a few years ago. Daddy is a successful businessman, a real self-made man. I've always idolized him, wanted to be like him. He's also an alcoholic. My mother is a school teacher and still has kids she taught years ago contact their "favorite teacher." She's a very special person. The divorce was not pretty, and both Mama and Daddy were devastated by it. Really devastated. Neither one could function. It was as if they loved each other, but couldn't live together and sadly enough, couldn't live without each other. Daddy's alcoholism brought out the worst in Mama, which created its own little vicious circle. The strange thing is that both are wonderful, good people. My family was utterly torn, yet somehow it made my older brother Terry, my younger sister Dana, and me all the more closer.

I never realized the horror of alcoholism while growing up. The problem had not gotten out of control until I was away from home at college. I had a great childhood and did not experience a dysfunctional atmosphere as a kid. Both of them gave me unconditional love.

But I saw a true picture of the alcoholism on a family ski trip to Park City, Utah in early 1995. Daddy must have gone through two or three huge bottles of vodka during the week we spent there. He could do little more than lie on the couch, and drink. It sickened all of us, but it was as if we were all numb, desensitized. We were afraid to say anything.

It took my little son James to say what we all felt.

"A. O., why do you drink so much alcohol?"

"That's none of your d___ business!" he shouted at James.

"Don't you talk to him like that!" Suzette yelled at Daddy. "He's just a little boy."

Daddy said some ugly things to her, and by that time my blood was boiling.

"You're nothing but a damn alcoholic," I screamed. "You've got no right to talk to my wife and child like that. I'm not going to stand for it."

It was the first time I had ever stood up to him. There wasn't a fight. The next morning as we were flying out of Park City, he was remorseful. He apologized and promised us that he would get some help. He had gone to a treatment center years before and had stayed sober for four or five years before succumbing again. That was what had precipitated the divorce.

Suzette didn't budge. She wouldn't even talk to him. I was proud of her. When we first began dating many years ago, she was shy, barely speaking. She's a beauty, but Suzette is also one of the brightest people I've ever met, and certainly one of the kindest. We're opposite in ways, me the extrovert, she the introvert; me the self-centered, hard charging, goal-oriented climber; she, the gentle, caring, giving "social chairman." She worries; I don't. But our strengths help the other's weaknesses. We have helped make each other a better person. We've had a great marriage, a strong one, one that

I'm proud of. Beneath Suzette's beautiful veneer was the real thing. She had a strength that most wouldn't see. She'd just proven her toughness to me.

We battled Daddy's sickness the entire year of 1995. Many times I thought he would die. His family physician Dr. David Thompson put him in the hospital in the late fall of 1995. He told me that Daddy's liver wouldn't take much more. He was developing cirrhosis. His blood pressure was going haywire. His face had a gray, death-like pallor. All of this was occurring while he was making more money than he'd ever made in his life — over a million dollars in one year. If money could have bought happiness, he could have. But it just doesn't work that way. I've never seen a more miserable man. Finally, in December of 1995 (around the time of the first dream) he entered another treatment facility in Baton Rouge.

During those first men's prayer group sessions in the spring of 1996, I poured my heart out about Daddy and Mama, hoping God could fix this problem. I knew I couldn't. My eyes weren't dry, and neither were my prayer partners'. Here I was, crying in front of other grown men. But it was this brokenness, not just from me but from the others too, that made this prayer group different.

I can't describe to you the great feeling I've received from the prayer group. It is almost like a narcotic. I had to have some of God's Spirit each week. If I missed Thursday morning, it made for a long week. I haven't missed much. Neither have the others. In fact, our numbers have steadily grown. We had many people becoming active, such as Mike King, Fred Lambert, my brother Terry, James and Stephen Dupont, David Knight, Myrt Hales, Ernie Greer, Mike Sullivan, Johnny B. Hoychick, Larry Tucker, Dan Lane, Perry

Pugh (our minister of youth), Gregg Bennett (our minister of music), Carlton Clark, and Hal Senn (Joe's brother). By the end of the summer, we consistently had twenty to twenty-five men there each prayer session. God was working among us, and we knew it. The church soon began to feel the impact of twenty-five men humbling themselves before God, pouring out their hearts and requests. And the prayers were bearing fruit — answers were being flashed before our eyes. But there was no quick and easy answer to my prayer for my father.

Joe Senn also gave us a warning. Satan didn't like what was going on and wasn't going to stand idly by while we were doing great things for God. He mentioned two verses:

1 Peter 5:8 (NIV)

> Be self-controlled and alert. Your enemy the devil prowls around like a roaring lion, looking for someone to devour.

Ephesians 6:11-12 (NIV)

> Put on the full armor of God, so that you can take your stand against the devil's schemes. For our struggle is not against flesh and blood, but against the rulers, against the authorities, against the powers of this dark world and against the spiritual forces of evil in the heavenly realms.

I would soon come under attack, as would others in the prayer group.

Chapter 3

THE SECOND DREAM

On the Fourth of July weekend of 1996, Suzette, the kids, and I traveled with my in-laws to Oakdale, Louisiana. Mrs. Sue's family — her mother and brother — live there. Uncle Don is a doctor. His son Todd is one of my closest friends and, like me, is an attorney. We had arrived on the evening of July 3rd at Grandma Nesom's house. On the trip down there, we always try to guess what dessert she has cooked. Any of them are great. The whole family gathered at Grandma's, and we talked well into the night. Suzette and I went to Uncle Don's house to sleep, by that time it was July 4th.

I closed my eyes that night, never expecting to have another supernatural experience.

I dreamed that I was in a room. It was crowded with people, as if a party was occurring. Against the far wall, I saw a man. He was leaning against it. It looked like something was wrong with him, as if he was mentally retarded. His head was bent at an awkward angle. One of his eyes was "cockeyed," straying off from the other. I walked across the room toward him. As I approached the man, he looked at me.

"**Twelve weeks**," he said.

Instantly, I knew it was related to the first dream. The face began to melt or peel away. Underneath, I could see a burnished or bronze skin. The after image was a face, a beautiful, perfect face almost like a statute, looking almost metallic.

This happened in seconds, and I instantly awoke. Just like before, I was "electrified." My heart was racing. I looked at my watch. It was around 3:00 a.m. My mind instantly filled with questions.

Was Jesus Christ returning in twelve weeks? What did the dream — now dreams— mean? That they were connected was undeniable. The feeling that dominated after the first dream was JOY. Incredible, undescribable joy. This second dream filled me with a sense of urgency.

If I thought I was frightened by the first dream, I was truly scared by the second. I didn't know what it meant. Was it a literal twelve weeks? Was it a message about the return of Christ or something else? Again, there were no angels or a voice from above to explain everything.

Like the first dream, I was struck by the vividness of the experience. I had slept and dreamed many times since the first one. Nothing religious. Nothing quite like the "electric" feeling I had upon waking up. I knew these were no ordinary dreams, but I was scared to think about it. In fact, I was so frightened by the second dream that I didn't tell anyone, not even Suzette. I just kept it to myself.

Chapter 4

PROMISE KEEPERS

Former Colorado football head coach Bill McCartney started an incredible movement in America. It began as a small group of men wanting to draw men back to God, back to their churches, and back to their families. A tiny spark can start a raging fire. Stadiums began to fill across the country. It was only a matter of time before it reached Louisiana. About eighteen men from our church went to a "wake-up" call in 1995 at Northeast Louisiana University. The wake-up call was a prelude to the "Big Show" in New Orleans on July 26-27, 1996. The message was simple. It was time for men to "wake up" and become men of God, men of integrity so lacking in the world today.

That message hit home in our church. Women had been doing most of the work for years. Mrs. Tut Bolton (the wife of George Bolton, Jr., the senior law partner in our firm) was the catalyst for many of the men to join in the "Experiencing God" study course. She even came before our deacon body asking us to participate. I'm glad that she did. Men have begun to wake up, including myself. The personal changes that have occurred in ordinary men's lives through Promise Keepers and the discipleship courses in our church have been remarkable. I've discussed Ricky Cooper. Rayland Trisler is another. Rayland was a year behind me in high school. We played football together. While I quarterbacked the team, Rayland was the starting tailback. Rayland was small, but tough as nails. He has an easy, infectious smile. Perhaps his strongest asset is his heart. I don't know if God grows them much bigger than Rayland's. In the prayer group, Rayland's heartfelt pleas bring tears to your eyes. It's an inspiration to see God's hand upon a man like Rayland. The change in his life wasn't some outlaw biker-into-preacher story. He was a Christian and a good man, but it's the difference between lukewarm and hot. And that makes all the difference in the world.

About eleven guys from our church made the trip to New Orleans for the Promise Keepers Conference in July of 1996 — Ricky Cooper and his son Ben, Wayne McManus, Ernie Greer, Rayland Trisler, Dan Lane, Carlton Clark, Bruce Parker and myself. Stephen and James Dupont came too, but didn't stay with us. I rode down with Bruce Parker and Dan Lane.

I had been to the Superdome many times for football games. I've got season tickets to the Saints games. This was a different group of saints gathered that weekend. The theme was "Breaking Down the Walls," a call to destroy the racial and denominational barriers dividing America, dividing the church. Never in my life have I experienced that Christ-centered unity that Promise Keepers seeks among men: black and white worshiping together, Baptist, Methodist, Catholic, Pentecostal, Presbyterian — you name the denomination, and it was represented there. I liked the purpose: to call men to reconcile with God, with their families, and with their fellow man.

Promise Keepers seeks to establish men of integrity and to send them back to their own communities to do God's work. The seven promises of a Promise Keeper are:

1. A Promise Keeper is committed to honor Jesus Christ through worship, prayer, and obedience to God's word in the power of the Holy Spirit.

2. A Promise Keeper is committed to pursue vital relationships with a few other men understanding that he needs brothers to help him keep his promises.

3. A Promise Keeper is committed to practice spiritual, moral, ethical, and sexual purity.

4. A Promise Keeper is committed to build strong marriages and families through love, protection, and biblical values.

5. A Promise Keeper is committed to support the mission of his church by honoring and praying for his pastor and by actively giving his time and resources.

6. A Promise Keeper is committed to reach beyond any racial and denominational barriers to demonstrate the power of biblical unity.

7. A Promise Keeper is committed to influence his world, being obedient to the Great Commandment (Mark 12:30-31) and the Great Commission (Matthew 28:19-20).

The two things I remember most from the weekend were Franklin Graham's sermon and a satellite hookup with Indianapolis, Indiana where another Promise Keeper's conference was going on. Graham is Billy Graham's son, heir apparent to that crusade empire. His sermon was short and to the point. A man's most valuable asset is his soul. What good does it do to gain the whole world but lose it? A good question. Later, the Indianapolis group was shown on the Superdome's big screens. We stood and sang "Amazing Grace" with almost 100,000 voices lifted to God. I leaned over to Bruce Parker and said, "We're getting a little taste of heaven today. Can you imagine what it's going to be like when we get there?" The sight of the thousands upon thousands of people gathered for Christ astonished me. It was a truly awesome sight. Unity. We were witnessing a living testament to a different world, one without racial or denominational differences.

Later that night, we were traveling home. Bruce and I were discussing the weekend's events. Dan Lane was in the back half asleep. I felt compelled to share about the dreams. Both of them. I discussed the visions at length.

"Look at my arms, I've got chill bumps," Bruce said, after I'd finished. "What does it mean?"

"I have no idea," I said. "I can't say that Jesus is coming in twelve weeks from July 4th. Thursday, September 26, 1996 is the date. I just know that I've gotten a sense of urgency from it. Joy from the first dream, but the second one gave me a feeling that something is about to happen." As we were talking, I remember Bruce flipping through several radio stations. He stopped on a strange sounding woman describing her visions of the Virgin Mary calling out to the church to repent because Christ is coming soon. Bruce and I just looked at each other. Chill bumps again.

Chapter 5

TWELVE WEEKS

What would you do if you knew the end of the world was coming, if Jesus was returning soon? Would you live differently? Would you make sure that the hearts of your family and friends were ready?

I can tell you what I did in response to the dreams.

Nothing.

After telling Bruce, I didn't say anything to anyone. Perhaps I rationalized it as just a dream. But I knew it wasn't. Ten weeks passed by quickly. In September I began a Bible study on Wednesday nights called "When God Speaks". This was a follow-up study to "Experiencing God". As we were in the second week of the Bible study, it brought to light some important questions for me.

When was the last time God spoke to you? How did you respond?

As I reflected on these questions, I felt terrible. God had spoken to me twice, and I had done nothing in response. There was a compulsion or need that welled up inside of me to share what had happened. Would people think I was crazy? Were the dreams biblical?

My first concern about sharing the dreams concerned the "twelve weeks." In Matthew 24:36,44 (NKJV), Jesus said (in speaking of the time of his return):

> But of that day and hour no one knows, no not even the angels of heaven, but My Father only ... Therefore, you also be ready, for the Son of Man is coming at an hour you do not expect.

These verses say that no one will know the day of Jesus' return. I wasn't even sure what the "twelve weeks" dream meant. I had always thought that people who "went up on the mountain" to wait for Jesus because some preacher thought it would be a certain day were misguided. No one knows the date and hour.

But I realized that I wasn't sharing the dreams because of a biblical concern. The real reason was that I was afraid. Afraid of what people would think. Afraid that they would think that I was crazy. Worried about my reputation. How would it affect my business, my precious standing in the community?

Things have always come easy to me. Academics, athletics, popularity. I graduated second in my class at Tulane. I have a growing, successful law practice. I had just turned thirty-three, and was seriously considering entering politics one day. I don't have a lot of skeletons in my closet, but this was all I needed.

"This guy's seeing visions," people would say. "Yeah, we really need to send him to Baton Rouge." Just the kind of thing that could keep me from being elected.

But my heart was telling me something else. God wanted me to share this. The question suddenly became "David, will you obey?" I thought back to the fifth reality of

Experiencing God: God speaking to you leads to a CRISIS OF BELIEF.

I felt like I was in a crisis.

I've always sought God on my own terms. Yes, God, I'll work for you; I'll serve you. But **don't** send me to Africa or take me out of my comfortable lifestyle and great job. I've been self-centered, doing what I wanted and hoping God approved.

He wanted me to share the dreams. He was wanting me to step off the side of a cliff and trust Him. I was scared to death. As I was traveling home from Monroe that afternoon, I made my decision.

"Lord, if You want me to say this, I'll say it — as crazy as it sounds. I'll obey You. Forgive me for wasting ten weeks before getting started. I just ask You to let me know that what I'm saying is true. Show me a sign that I'm doing right. I don't want to say anything false, and I know You don't want me saying anything wrong or that would lead someone astray. Show me a sign."

The scary thing about prayer is that we sometimes get what we ask for.

That evening, on September 11, I told the people in our study group about the two dreams. My voice was trembling and my heart was pounding. I was a professional speaker, normally smooth as silk, calm as a glass lake. But not that night.

I bared my soul for all to see. I stepped off the precipice, and it was the greatest decision I've ever made. I emphasized to them that I didn't know what the dreams meant. I didn't know if Jesus was coming on September 26th. What I **could** say was what had happened to me, what I had experienced. And the emotions I felt. Extreme joy at the first. Extreme urgency from the second.

I felt relieved once I had finished. I could tell it had made an impact. Afterwards, Rayland Trisler caught me on the way to the church service. Rayland had not been in the Bible study group. He had something he wanted me to read. Rayland had heard about the dream from Bruce Parker. He passed me a photocopy of "The Prophecy Club Newsletter". It told of Bob Wadsworth who had charted certain celestial events that pointed to the beginning of the tribulation period on **September 26/27, 1996**, with something significant happening in Israel on that date. According to the newsletter, Israel would be attacked soon thereafter. I normally don't put too much credence in these types of doomsday publications, but now my head was swimming. September 26 was the exact date of the end of the twelve weeks. It was almost too much to believe. Shortly after praying for a sign, here was Rayland handing me this newsletter out of the blue.

When I got home, Suzette and I sat down and discussed everything for the first time. I could tell it frightened her.

"What do you think it means, David?"

"I don't know."

"This is scary. I can hardly breathe."

The phone rang and I answered it. No one was on the line.

"That must be our mystery caller," I said. We had recently been receiving a number of hang-up calls.

The phone rang again. I picked it up. It was Suzette's dad, Mr. Jimmy.

"Did y'all just call here?" he asked.

"No, sir."

"Well, we just had a phone call, but when I answered no one was there. Your number was on the caller ID box."

"What?"

"Your number was on the caller ID box."

"Are you sure?"

"Yeah. Do you think one of the kids snuck in the kitchen and called?"

"I don't know. Hold on. I'll check."

Our kids love "Mamie" and "Poppa". Often, they will go into the kitchen and call their grandparents without our knowing. I walked to their rooms. Both were sound asleep. I returned to the phone.

"Nope. They're asleep. This is pretty weird. We just had a hang-up call right before you called."

After I got off the phone, I told Suzette. Smiling, I hummed the theme to the Twilight Zone.

"This is just too bizarre," Suzette said. That was a phrase that would be repeated quite often in our household during the next two weeks.

The next day after work, Suzette and I continued to talk about these things. She had been busy. She went to see her mother in Delhi and told her about the dreams. She wanted to make sure that her parents were ready. She also discussed it with her sister in Fort Worth. The urgency was in her to make sure her family was ready. Just in case.

I had also been busy. I shared the dreams with our men's prayer group on that Thursday morning. Terry and I discussed it at work. I also told my secretary Rosie, my paralegal Bevie Lee, and my law partner Tom Allen. I prefaced it with "You're probably going to think I'm crazy." Each time I shared it, it was a blessing. It felt right.

Terry wanted to know what I really thought it meant. The two of us are more than just brothers; we're also best friends. We run together, work together, and do most things together. He wanted to know what I really thought, not just what I was telling everyone. That day at lunch I had watched CNN. The news of the Middle East unrest and Saddam Hussein disturbed me. That, combined with the Prophecy Club Newsletter, made me feel very uneasy about the safety of Israel. I told both Terry and Tom this. I was afraid. Israel may be attacked on September 26. That was my gut reaction.

I also spoke again to my law partner Johnny Hoychick. Johnny has been a real mentor to me, one of the best attorneys I've ever met and certainly one of the wisest men I've ever known. He's a very strong Christian man, a leader of our church.

"Maybe God is telling you something else. Maybe it's not about the Second Coming, but a test. Remember Abraham. God told him to sacrifice his beloved son. It was a test for Abraham to see if he would obey. God demands our obedience. Maybe he's seeing if you will say what He wants you to."

After work, Suzette and I continued to talk about the visions. I went for a three mile run, just to get my mind off everything. It didn't work. As I ran, I continued to pray that God would show me that this was the right thing to do. When I made it back to the house, Suzette was waiting.

"Go look at my Bible."

"What do you mean?"

"Just go look at my Bible. When you were gone I opened it. Go see. David, this is just too weird."

I went and looked. It was opened to the first chapter of Jeremiah. This passage details how God knew Jeremiah even before He formed him in the womb. That He had ordained Jeremiah to be a prophet. Jeremiah had tried to make excuses that he was too young. God said, "Don't be afraid. I am with you to deliver you."

"Are you supposed to be some kind of prophet?" Suzette asked.

"I don't think so, but I don't know what's in store. All I know is that I'm supposed to share it. What if Jesus does come in two weeks and I never said anything? Regardless of what happens, this has been a blessing to me. I've learned a real lesson in obedience. This is the first time I've really stood up for Christ. The first time I've gotten off the fence. It feels good."

Suzette said it had also blessed her. Her thoughts were more focused on Jesus. She was thinking about Him all day long. She had been reading her Bible, and she had a closeness that she hadn't felt in a long time.

"Did you put up that sign?" she asked suddenly.

"What sign?"

"You mean you didn't put it up? What about Rayland?"

"What are you talking about?"

"You really didn't put it up?"

"No, what is it?"

"As I came off the interstate from Delhi, there was a sign on a telephone pole right in front of me. It said '**Repent. Jesus is coming immediately**.'

Later that night we went to the Sonic for a bite to eat. I saw my mother, Jenny Doughty. She got into the car with us, and I shared with her about the dreams and all of the strange things that were happening.

Mama told me that she once had a dream of heaven and had seen her father "Daddy Ford" fishing there. This wasn't the only time that someone I told about the dreams shared with me things they had experienced. It seemed to me that I wasn't alone. Many people had similar experiences.

Only like me, they hadn't shared it with others. When the food arrived, the Sonic waitress said, "That'll be seven dollars and seventy-seven cents."

$7.77. Seven, seven, seven.

"That's the holy number," Mama said. We had recently studied in Sunday school about the mark of the beast in Revelation - 666. It was a sign of evil, incompleteness, perfect evil. In the Bible, seven was the number of completeness, the holy number.

"See what I mean," Suzette said. "This is just **too** weird."

Chapter 6

THE LAST WEEK

On Saturday, September 21, an old college friend Marcus Murphy called. Marcus had recently became the pastor at the First Baptist Church in Delhi. He was calling to see if I knew someone who could preach for him the next morning. He had a ruptured disc in his back that would eventually require surgery. Instead of seizing the opportunity to share the dreams with an entire congregation, I let it slip through my fingers. I suggested several names and even told Marcus that if he wanted me to, I would speak. When he hung up, I knew that I hadn't done right. I should have told him not to worry about it, that I would do it. Here I was getting puffed up that I was doing such a good job for God and obeying, and now I had fallen flat on my face.

I woke up early Sunday morning and began work on a sermon just in case Marcus had to fall back on me. When it got to be a decent hour, I gave him a call. The line was busy. Finally, I reached him. He had just gotten someone else to do it. He didn't need me.

I was relieved to a degree, but I could help but think that I had missed the boat.

When I arrived at the office early Monday morning on September 23, I already had a phone message from Dr. Lamar Lane. I called him back.

"Did you see the sunrise this morning?" Lamar asked.

"Nope. I was up, but didn't see it."

"It was the most spectacular sunrise I've ever seen. Blood red. It makes you think."

"I wish I'd seen it."

"David, what do you think the dreams really mean?"

Everyone was asking the same question.

"I don't know, Lamar. My gut reaction is that something's going to happen to Israel. Maybe it'll be attacked."

"Did you know there's going to be a lunar eclipse on the 26th?"

"An eclipse?" I could feel the chill bumps rise again.

"Yeah. A total eclipse of the moon."

We talked some more about the strange events that had been occurring. Later I also called Bruce Parker about it.

"Regardless of what happens, David," Bruce said, "even if nothing happens, this has really been a blessing in my life. It's gotten me closer to God. I think about Him more. I've even shared this with some people at work."

I felt the same way.

Later that same day, I told some of our secretaries (the ones I hadn't already told) about the dreams and what was happening. One of them, Cindy Odom, began to cry. She hadn't been in church for several years. She had begun to question her salvation. Before work that morning she had prayed that God would show her an answer and tell her what to do. She had overheard the conversation between Lamar and me and had gone into the bathroom and asked Christ into her heart. There wasn't a dry eye in our office. It was incredible what God was doing.

On Tuesday, September 24, my schedule was cleared for the rest of the week. It was supposed to have been a very hectic week with a trial on Wednesday and another on Thursday. One case settled and the other was postponed.

Was God giving me this opportunity to tell others?

I had spoken to almost everyone in my immediate family with one big exception. My father. Late Tuesday afternoon I left work and drove to his office. My sister Dana was there, but Daddy wasn't.

"He hasn't called you?" she asked.

"Nope."

"He's in the hospital again."

"Hospital! Where?"

“Here in Rayville. Dr. Thompson put him in. His drinking has been getting worse and worse."

After Daddy had gotten out of the treatment center in Baton Rouge the past December, he had been doing a lot better. But I had been hearing rumors that he was drinking again. It seemed like a never-ending battle.

As I drove to the hospital, I cut on the radio. The

same song was playing again. Every time I had gotten into the car that day, the same song had been playing on the Christian radio station I was listening to. It was called "People Get Ready" by Crystal Lewis.

"People get ready; Jesus is coming; soon we'll be going home..." The song wouldn't go away. Neither would its message.

When I arrived at the hospital, I was nervous. How would Daddy react to what I said? Well, there was nothing to lose.

"Daddy, I've got something to tell you," I said when I saw him in the hospital room.

"So do I," he said.

I discussed the dream with him. Tears came into his eyes after I had finished.

"Daddy, I want to make sure your heart is right with Jesus. I'm not sure what the twelve weeks means, but I don't want to take any chances."

"I think I know what it means," Daddy said. "That if I don't get straightened out, I'm going to die. I gave my heart to Jesus a long time ago, was baptized in the old church building y'all have just renovated. I haven't been living right, but I know that I'm saved. He's been watching over me for a long time, even with all of these problems."

"Why do you think the dreams mean you're going to die?" I asked.

"Your first dream was in December at the same time I was in the treatment center. You remember that before I went, Dr. Thompson told me that if I kept on drinking, I was going to die. My liver was enlarged and developing cirrhosis." He paused. "There are some things that I've never told you that I've experienced — of a similar nature as yours. When I was about five or six, I almost died eating a blackberry that they thought had spider eggs in it. I remember it just like it was yesterday, lying in my sister's arms. Then, suddenly I was in the brightest light I've ever seen. It was the best feeling in the world."

"I can relate to that," I said with a smile.

"I heard someone say that it 'wasn't my time', and the next thing I know, I was back in my sister's arms. They thought I had really died for a short period of time."

"Daddy, I'd like to ask you something. We have a men's prayer group on Thursday mornings. I'd like for you to come, so we can pray over you. I think it would do some good."

"I think it would too. I've been trying to fight this problem by myself for too long. I need to take a different approach. I need to turn it over to God."

"It's nothing strange or crazy. We'll just put a hand on you and pray for God to take this problem away from you and away from our family."

"I'll do it. They're supposed to let me out of here today or tomorrow afternoon."

"What did the doctor say?"

"You're not going to believe it. My liver was getting worse and worse last year. My blood pressure was too high. All because of the drinking. Since I've been in, Dr. Thompson has checked me out. He came in here earlier and laid all of the test results on the bed. Everything was normal. Liver, fine. Blood pressure, fine. It's a miracle."

"Maybe God is trying to get your attention, Daddy. Maybe there's something he wants you to do. Just think what a testimony an A. O. Doughty-on-fire-for-the-Lord would be."

"I've thought about that. Maybe so. I don't know what He's got in mind, but maybe so."

As I left the hospital, I could barely contain my excitement. I was thrilled that Daddy was going to come to the prayer group. Maybe it was the breakthrough we had been looking for. After dinner that night, I decided to pray and fast the next day. Now, I've never missed three meals in a row my entire life, but something told me it was necessary.

Wednesday, September 25

I spoke that morning to several of the prayer group members: Joe Senn, Dr. Winburn, and Ricky Cooper. I told them about Daddy and that he was going to be at the prayer group so we could pray over him. They all committed to be there.

At about 10:00 a.m., Daddy showed up at the office. I could tell he was excited about something. He sat down across the desk from me.

"Something happened to me last night. I spent about half the night in prayer. I asked God to take away the alcohol from me. It felt as if some tremendous burden was lifted off of me. I haven't felt this good in years. He took it away from me." Daddy's voice was trembling, his eyes full of tears.

He also had some bad news. My aunt Esther (the sister who had held him when he almost died) was in the hospital. She had multiple health problems: her heart, kidneys, and circulation in her leg. Daddy said the doctors didn't give her much chance to make it. He was probably going to have to leave today.

"I knew something would come up, Daddy. Satan doesn't want you there tomorrow morning."

"Well, David, I can't just neglect my sister on her deathbed."

"I understand that, but I think it's just another obstacle being thrown in the way."

"If I can make it, I promise you I'll be there," Daddy said.

He left, but I was a bit discouraged. At lunch I went to the house. Suzette was gone. Instead of eating, I prayed by a couch. I asked God to take care of Aunt Esther and that Daddy would be able to be at the prayer group on Thursday. I thanked and praised God for the dreams and letting me see Him, firsthand, at work. It had been an incredible inspiration in my life. I prayed so long that I fell asleep.

Perry Pugh, our youth minister, had asked me to share the visions with the youth at Wednesday church. At 5:30 p.m. I told a group of about twenty-five to thirty young people about the dreams. From their faces, I couldn't tell if it had affected them or not. I just told the story and left, returning to the "When God Speaks" Bible study group. In the class, we discussed how God was at work in our community. Myrt Hales, another attorney in town, related what had happened to him earlier that day. His client, an elderly woman, had given a deposition, and he was discussing afterwards the estimated time to trial, etc. He told her it may take a year before it ever went to trial.

"Don't worry about it then," she said.

"What do you mean?"

"I'm not going to be here in a year."

He still didn't understand her. "Are you going to die?"

"My preacher's wife has had a vision. Jesus is coming again, this year. I'm not going to be here."

After church that night, Perry Pugh caught me. Three youths had been saved at their meeting. I barely caught my breath. Miracles were happening. We were actually seeing the hand of God at work. It was an awesome sight.

Thursday, September 26

I awoke easily at 5:25 a.m. to get ready for the men's prayer group meeting. I didn't sleep real well. To say I was anxious would be a drastic understatement. What was going to happen today? Was Jesus returning? Would Israel be attacked? Would Daddy show up?

I was also wondering if I would even be alive after the 26th. The thought had certainly entered my mind that the dreams may have meant that I had only twelve weeks to live. But I hadn't said this to anyone, especially Suzette.

At the church, I arrived early for the prayer session. Ricky was there, too. In just a few minutes, I saw Daddy at the door. I can't tell you how proud I was of him. For a man of his pride to humble himself and come was itself a miracle. We had an especially large group that morning. We split into smaller groups. About seven or eight of us prayed for Daddy. These were powerful, sincere prayers to God in praise for what He was doing, what He was about to do in taking the demon of alcohol away from Daddy. There wasn't a dry eye among these men. I've learned a truth. Real men cry. Real men are broken to God.

It was an especially great time for my brother Terry and me. We had struggled with the alcoholism for so long. For us to witness Daddy praying there with us was almost too much.

Terry and I went to get some breakfast after the prayer time. I was starving. My fast was over. Terry asked me, "Did you hear the news this morning?"

"No."

"It's Israel. They've had the worst fighting in the Gaza Strip in years. A lot of people were killed. Can you believe it? An attack in Israel on September 26th. It had something to do with a tunnel near the Wailing Wall and a Muslim Mosque."

We got into the car. I had previously told Terry about the Crystal Lewis song "People Get Ready" and how it was on every time I was in the car. I turned on the ignition. Crystal Lewis was bellowing out, "People get ready; Jesus is coming; soon we'll be going home."

Terry stared at me.

"I don't want to get on that airplane," he said. He was scheduled to fly to Houston for a deposition later that day. I didn't blame him.

As I was working later that morning, Cindy Odom rushed into the office.

"David, you're not going to believe this. I just got off the phone with Cody. Several of the cheerleaders at the junior high school were talking about your dream and four people at the school were saved."

My mother, a fifth grade teacher at Rayville Elementary, also called me that day from school and told me the same thing happened there. Young kids sharing and praying for one another. Four more children had accepted the Lord.

I had to pinch myself to make sure I wasn't dreaming. Could this all be happening at the same time? Eleven kids saved in less than twenty-four hours?

That day Tom Allen called from his car phone. He and his dad were on vacation on his way to Venice, Louisiana for a fishing trip.

"Did you see the paper?"

"No, but Terry told me about Israel."

"No. I'm talking about page 10A of the *News-Star World*?"

"What does it say?"

"Just look at it. I'll call you later."

Near an article concerning the attack in the Gaza Strip and a report on the lunar eclipse, an advertisement discussed "The Soon Approach of Jesus Christ's Return". It listed evidence that the "soon" return of Jesus Christ was overwhelming. I'd never seen an ad like it before or since. Neither had Tom.

Later that evening, I went to my grandmother's house, "Mama" Pearl Ware. I had learned the Bible at her feet. She was a devout woman of God with as much Bible knowledge, and probably more, than any preacher in the area. She had been to the Holy Land countless times. Maybe she could make some sense of all of this.

I told her about the visions and the strange events following in their wake.

"God has spoken to you, David. And it's obvious that you are doing what He wants you to do — telling others about it. No one can deny that the Holy Spirit has been at work with all of those lives saved."

"Well, I haven't done too good of a job. I waited ten weeks to get started. What if Jesus does return today? I should have told a lot more people than I have."

"But you don't know that's what it means."

"No, much of it has already been fulfilled. The uprising in Israel. Daddy's miracle. The lives that have been saved. Even if nothing else happens, this has been the most incredible thing that's ever happened to me."

Mama Pearl discussed several things about Christ's return. She talked about First Thessalonians, chapter 4, and that the dead in Christ would rise first. Then it hit me.

"Mama Pearl, I've never thought about that. The red cloud that I saw in the first dream was directly over where the Masonic Cemetery is located."

Driving back from Mama Pearl's, the sky was cloudy, just as it had been in the first dream. Was today the day?

Later that night, I watched the lunar eclipse — the last full one of this century. It was overcast in Rayville, but I could see it occasionally through a break in the clouds. The moon had a reddish hue. Tom Allen called me back from New Orleans, talking about the moon turning blood red.

> The sun will be turned to darkness
> and the moon to blood
> before the coming of the great and
> dreadful day of the LORD.
>
> Joel 2:31 (NIV)

I had about ten calls that night from various friends. Terry even called from Houston. Everyone was excited. I also watched CNN. The headline stories on the night of September 26, 1996, give an interesting picture of our world and perhaps its future:

(1) The deaths and disturbance in the Gaza Strip, the tunnel in Jerusalem, and the threat of war in the Middle East.

(2) Richard Allen David, the convicted murderer of a small girl, Polly Klaus, was sentenced to death. He had barbarically tortured the girl before she died. He had absolutely no remorse over the death, even accusing the girl's father of molestation with his last breath in court.

(3) The last full lunar eclipse of the century. A meteorologist explained that dust particles in the atmosphere gave it a reddish tint.

(4) Congress failed to override President Clinton's veto by nine votes. This would allow late term abortions — a controversial manner of killing the fetus.

(5) Two hurricanes were brewing in the oceans of the world.

Chapter 7

THE THIRD DREAM

Of course, Jesus didn't return on September 26, 1996. But some pretty amazing things did happen. And they have continued to occur. The ripple effects are still moving through our community. Dan Lane, an assistant principal at the junior high school, has seen the students form a prayer group, with over sixty kids in attendance. Dan has also been instrumental in forming a Richland Parish Promise Keepers group. People are drawing nearer to God and spending more time reading the Bible.

On October 2, I called Suzette's cousin Todd Nesom about the dreams and all of the incredible events. After I told him about the dreams, Todd could barely talk.

"I'm flushed," he said. "David, I haven't been living right. Sure, I haven't been stealing or killing anybody, but we're not going to church. I've been living for myself. I've gone through some rocky times lately. Maybe God is teaching me a lesson now — telling me to get my life right."

"What about Hallie?" I asked. "The whole time y'all have been married, I've never had a spiritual discussion with her. What's the state of her heart?"

Todd paused. "I don't know. But I'm going to call her tonight. She's out of town."

The next morning I spoke to Uncle Don, Todd's father.

He appreciated me speaking to Todd. He had eaten breakfast with him, and Todd had told him that he had spoken to Hallie. They had cried over the phone and prayed together. Both had decided to become active in the local church, something Uncle Don and Aunt Bev had been trying to do for some time. Todd also called me back. He said that after he had spoken to Hallie, he went to eat supper at some friends' house. He told them he had really decided to change his lifestyle and start putting God first. He had not mentioned the dreams. The friend told him about a dream she had recently experienced that had made a change in her. It was of Armageddon. Wars, destruction, death.

"David, chill bumps ran up my spine. Then I told her about your dreams. It was pretty strange."

"I'm getting used to it now, Todd. Welcome to the Twilight Zone."

About one week later, in the early hours of October 10, 1996, I had the third dream.

A large group of people were in the Sunday school class I teach at First Baptist, although the room looked different from the one we normally meet in. Each week we close in prayer, joining hands with one another in a circle. I was standing in the circle beside David Head. I've know David for most of my life, growing up playing baseball with him since I was a kid. He is married to my first cousin Lora, and has had to deal with some of the same alcohol problems in his family that I've had. As he was praying, David began to cry and pray for his parents. Soon, everyone in the room started crying, and we continued to pray for quite some time. We were running late for the church service, but we kept on praying.

Afterwards, we left the building, moving outside. It didn't look like the exact scene outside our church, but was more open, giving us a better view of the sky. In the distance, I could see "holes" opening up in the clouds overhead. Unlike the first dream with its reddish clouds, these were pillars of light, much like when sunlight breaks through a cloud. These shafts of light began opening up across the sky. Everywhere. It was an awesome sight.

"I hope it's not about to happen," I heard a voice say behind me. It was Greg Hogue, a member of the Sunday school class.

Above me I saw some swirling shapes. Circles. Each looked like a funnel cloud twisting in a perfect circle as if a hole were about to open up directly above us. The circles were arranged in a geometric pattern. I recognized it immediately. A six-pointed star. The Star of David. Then I noticed that all of the shafts of light across the sky were arranged in a similar pattern.

Suddenly, I felt myself pulled upward, racing toward the clouds. I didn't know if it was real or a dream. I clutched the side of the bed, grabbing the mattress. Suddenly, I awoke, just as I was about to enter the clouds.

My heart was thundering in my chest again. The same "electrified" feeling was back. I glanced at the clock beside the bed. 3:00 a.m. All of the dreams had occurred at about the same time of night.

"Suzette?"

"Yeah," she said groggily.

"I had another dream."

"You're kidding."

"No. It just happened." I held up my hand. It was still shaking. I described the dream to her.

"David, you're just thinking of things that happened. Last night we had gotten into deep conversation about religious things just before we went to bed. And we put glow-in-the dark stars on James' ceiling." Leave it to the resident skeptic to take the wind out of the sails.

"It wasn't even the same shaped star," I argued. "This one had six points. The Star of David. Like on Israel's flag. And I've had a bunch of dreams since this began, but none like these three with my heart pounding and my hands shaking. Just because we were talking about religious things before we went to sleep isn't extraordinary. Hey, for the past month, that's about all I've had on my mind. But I didn't have any more dreams until now."

She held me.

"I'm sorry. I don't disbelieve you. It just scares me to death."

I lay awake the rest of the night pondering the meaning of the latest dream. It was Thursday morning, and I got up early at 5:25 for the men's prayer group. I was soon to find out it was going to be quite a meeting.

We had a large crowd at the prayer group that morning, including Wanda Sharbono. She had been at one of our meetings a few months before as she was trying to form a women's prayer group at our church. She had come to share something with us.

"Some of you may know that on August 22nd, I came here to your meeting. I asked you to pray for me." Wanda went on to tell that she had been diagnosed with multiple sclerosis. She hadn't told anyone. She was scared to death, but had been praying for God to heal her. She said that on Thursday, August 22nd, she came to our prayer group and we had prayed for her. Three days later, the symptoms disappeared. She hasn't had any since. The doctors are still shocked.

"If you've never seen a living miracle, you're looking at one," she said. We all prayed and thanked God for His blessings and for Wanda. We thanked Him for letting us see His hand at work. Afterward, I shared with them about the third dream.

"David, I'm not an interpreter of dreams," Joe Senn said after I had finished, "but the Star of David symbolizes God's chosen people. I believe that we as Christians are God's chosen people today. The light also fascinates me. I've always imagined as I'm driving around down the road and see sunlight break through a cloud that we'll be taken up in that kind of scene."

Joe continued to speak.

"We've been talking about miracles this morning, and I have something to share with you guys. I've been preaching a revival at Dunn Baptist Church. I was amazed at how the youth were touched by the Holy Spirit."

Joe went on to describe how two young girls—sisters—began to pray for their father during the week—long revival. They would stay at the altar pleading with God to save him. Within a few days, their father came to a worship service and ended up giving his life to the Lord. Then the sisters began to work on their grandfather, someone who hadn't darkened the door to a church for many years. Joe and the local pastor even went by to see him, but he refused to talk with them. But the girls kept on praying and trying to talk to their grandfather. Before the week was over, he, too, had come to church, walked the aisle and had been saved.

But that wasn't all ... the girls had tried to get a friend of theirs to come to church on Sunday to hear the revival. The young man told them that he couldn't. He was going fishing. The next day at school, the girls asked him to come Monday evening. Again the boy said that as soon as school was out, he was headed to the fishing hole.

"Well, I guess we're just going to have to pray that God messes up your fishing trip," one of the girls said.

Later, the young man went fishing. His boat sank. That night Joe saw him sitting on the second row from the front. The boy was saved that night.

"God is working in a powerful way in our community, men," Joe said. "He is pouring out His Spirit on us. I've never seen anything like it." Even the older men in our group admitted the same. They had never seen such an outpouring of the Holy Spirit. Nothing even close.

I wondered, was this something happening only in a remote area of northeast Louisiana or was this type of thing happening all over the world?

> And afterward, I will pour out my Spirit on all people.. I will pour out my Spirit in those days...before the coming of the great and dreadful day of the LORD.
>
> Joel 2:28, 29, 31 (NIV)

I spoke to David Head a short time afterward on a Saturday afternoon. I didn't know if the dream had some special meaning to him, but I felt as though I needed to tell him. David and Lora were certainly startled by what I said. It must be strange to wind up in someone else's dream, especially in this situation.

The next day, Sunday morning, David had yet another strange "coincidence." He was reading the Sunday *News-Star World* when he came across an article written by Greg Miller, a local pastor. The article detailed the two full lunar eclipses (both very red in color) that had occurred in 1996, the first on April 4 and the second on September 26. Lunar eclipses are extremely rare, much rarer than solar eclipses. Oddly enough, both of these occurred on or near Jewish holidays. April 4 was the Jewish Passover, which commemorates when the Angel of Death "passed over" the Jewish household to kill the first born of the Egyptians during Moses' time. The second red lunar eclipse on September 26 was just after Yom Kippur, the Jewish Day of Atonement. It's a day of confession, repentance, and prayers for forgiveness for sins committed during the year. That entire week is a holy week and ends with Sukkoth, the Feast of Tabernacle or Tents. It is the last holy day of the Jewish year and commemorates the forty- year sojourn in the wilderness, living in tents. Another partial lunar eclipse occurred on March 23, 1997, on yet another Jewish holiday — the Feast of Purim. This near total eclipse was also red in color. It also happened to be Palm Sunday, when Christ made his triumphant entry into Jerusalem shortly before His crucifixion. Greg Miller made the following observation in the article:

"If three red moons don't get your attention as a biblical sign, what will? Someone being raised from the dead?"

I also spoke to Greg Hogue, who had made the statement in the third dream that "I hope it's not about to happen." He and David Head were the only people I could distinctly remember after waking up. Greg, an insurance salesman, was at the law office one day working on some cancer policies for us. I discussed the dreams with him, and in particular, the last one.

"I don't know if it has any special meaning to you, but I wanted to tell you about it."

Greg thanked me for sharing the dreams with him.

"David, I don't know what it all means, but I can tell you that I've been really burdened about my children. Austin has been saved, but Jordan and Bailey haven't. Both of them are certainly old enough to know. She's thirteen and he's ten. If something happened right now, I don't know if they'd go to heaven. I'd appreciate it if you could pray for them. I've been praying about it a lot."

Within two months of our talk, Bailey Hogue came forward at one of our church services and was later baptized.

God hears us when we cry out. We often think that He's distant, not caring about us. But the startling truth that I was learning, that He was teaching me, was that He **does** hear. He listens. He certainly heard a father's prayers for his son.

Chapter 8

I AM NOT ALONE

Tom Allen, one of my law partners and very close friends, had been incredibly excited by what was happening. He had tipped me off to the odd advertisement on page 10A of the *News Star World* on September 26th. The ad had said to write for a free report concerning "Angels Announce Christ's Soon Return."

I had immediately sent a letter requesting the report. A few months later, it arrived. The report detailed events that happened in 1993 to a chemist named Vincent Tam in Tennessee. The account was verified by the man's pastor as well as other reputable men in the community as to Vincent's character. Vincent was of Chinese descent, born in Singapore. On Thursday, March 25, 1993, Vincent was working late in his laboratory. At 1:30 a.m. he looked out of a window and saw a man standing by the passenger side door of his car. Thinking the man was trying to steal his vehicle, Vincent rushed to the parking lot, carrying an 18-inch metal rod. He was also proficient in Chi-Sao, a form of martial art.

"Hi, can I help you?" Vincent said as cheerfully as he could, keeping the rod hidden behind his back. The stranger was of medium build, with clean cut, straight hair. He was wearing jeans, T-shirt, and white tennis shoes.

"Hi, Vincent."

"Do I know you?"

"Not really."

"Who are you?" Vincent asked suddenly.

"I have the same name of your primary and secondary school." He paused. "I'm a friend. You don't have to use Chi-Sao or the rod on me."

Vincent was startled. No one, not even his best friend in the U.S., knew about his Chi-Sao skills. His primary and secondary school was back in Singapore. **St. Gabriel.**

"How do you know that?"

"I know," the stranger replied. "By the way, Mum is fine." Mum was Vincent's mother who had recently suffered heart complications, and he had been very concerned about her.

"You love the Lord very much, don't you?" Gabriel continued.

"That's right," Vincent said.

"He loves you very much, too," Gabriel paused. "He's coming **very, very soon**." He emphasized the last words.

Then he asked,"Can I have a cup of water?"

"Sure." Vincent turned to get the water, but decided to ask the stranger inside to drink from the water fountain. When Vincent turned back, Gabriel was gone. He had suddenly vanished in an almost completely vacant parking lot.

Vincent had several other experiences, each confirming

the information that Jesus was going to be returning very, very soon.

The report also discussed the experience of David Gant of Bryant, Alabama, a business owner in his early thirties. He was scuba diving and became lost in a series of underwater river caves on August 15-16, 1992. With his air supply limited, David found a small, eighteen-inch high air pocket. Clinging to a stalactite, he realized that he was going to die after fourteen exhausting hours of trying to hang on. David was not a church-goer, but in desperation he prayed for the Lord to save his soul. He instantly felt a hand go inside of him, pulling out the evil within.

"As it came out, I've never felt cleaner, better or happier in all of my life."

David was so joyful that he begged the Lord not to take him so he could tell others. Then he heard a distinct voice:

"I want you to go and get your family ready to meet me. Go tell the whole world that I am coming back for my children before the year 2000."

David then saw a vision of his rescue and telling the rescuers of his "message". Now David had peace and confidence. He clung to the stalactite for another six hours before his eventual rescue. David's life has totally changed. Now he shares this message in various churches and meetings.

Tom and I were startled by the report. We had discussed that maybe God was showing the same message to others around the world. Deep down, I felt that if my dreams indicated Christ's return, surely He wasn't telling only a thirty-three year old country boy in rural northeast Louisiana. As I was finding out, I was not alone.

God is at work around us, speaking to people, shouting a warning.

"People get ready; Jesus is comin; Soon we'll be going home."

Problem is, the world isn't listening.

Chapter 9

THE DREAMS CONTINUE

On Wednesday, January 22, 1997, Bruce Parker and I were talking after our Bible study group.

"Have you had any more dreams?" he asked.

"Nope. It's been about three months."

"I have to admit that I've lost my edge. Things were so intense just before September 26. Now with water under the bridge, it's sort of gone."

"I've lost my edge, too." I paused. "You know, I used to think how stupid those Israelites were. God had performed all of those incredible miracles in delivering them out of Egypt. They'd seen the Red Sea part, but just as soon as they got to Mount Sinai and Moses was gone for awhile, they forgot. They turned away from God and worshiped a golden calf. Now I can identify with them. I've literally seen the hand of God move. He's spoken to me, vividly through a series of dreams. I've seen miracles. Now only three months later, time has dulled it, as if it's only a distant memory. That really bothers me."

Later that same evening, Lamar Lane also approached me.

"Any more dreams?"

I shook my head. "Not in awhile."

That same night I had another dream, in the early morning hours of January 23. As with the others, it was so vivid I didn't realize I was dreaming.

It was a dreary day, overcast, damp and drizzling rain. I was walking from my law office down Madeline Street past the Richland Parish Courthouse. In my hand was an opened umbrella. The rain was too heavy to walk without one, but too light to really need one. As I walked, I studied the overcast sky, with its patches of dark clouds. Several tiny breaks allowed shafts of light to filter through.

Since the dreams first began, I've often found myself staring at the sky in anticipation. When was it going to happen? Would I be alive to see it? A cloudy sky had special meaning to me now. It is a constant reminder.

As I walked down Madeline Street, staring at the sky, the same thoughts hit me.

"The sky looks a lot like it did in the dreams," I thought.

Continuing walking, I suddenly felt myself lifted upwards, umbrella and all. As I shot into the sky, I awoke, my senses tingling.

"Suzette, I've had another dream," I rolled over and said.

She didn't comment. It was 5:00 a.m.

Doubts began to assail me. Had I triggered the dream

simply because Bruce and Lamar had asked me about it earlier that evening? Although it was similar, it somehow "felt" different. The electricity wasn't as intense. The time of the morning was different. Was it just my imagination?

As I showered that morning before going to the Thursday morning Men's prayer group, I decided that I wasn't going to tell anyone. I was going to keep this one to myself. That determination was still with me when I arrived at the church. The room was packed with almost thirty men gathered to pray. As I sat quietly listening to the prayer requests, my heart began to pound. I was short of breath. It was as if God were putting His thumb on me.

"I've given you visions to share. I want you to spit it out," He seemed to be telling me.

Well, I spit it out, although reluctantly. After our prayer session, several guys approached me. Each of them told me how much it meant to hear about the dreams and how it had renewed their spirits.

It had done the same thing for me. It was as if God was carefully, purposefully reminding me.

"David, don't forget about this. I'm serious. The dreams have a clear message. Jesus will be coming soon."

Of course, there was no actual voice, but this was the message I felt in my heart. God was tapping me on the shoulder.

"Don't forget, David. Don't forget."

Chapter 10

THE LAST TIME

Exactly one month later, on Sunday, February 23, 1997, I had the fifth dream. That Saturday evening, Suzette and I had gone to the Stephen Curtis Chapman concert with Lamar and Gaye Lane and Todd and Lori Morris. As we were leaving, Lamar asked me a question.

"Have you seen the comet?"

"What comet?"

"Hale-Bopp. Jimmy Posey told me about it. You can see it in the sky in the east about an hour or an hour and a half before sunrise. Supposedly, there is some type of bright object traveling with it. No one knows what it is."

That night I fell asleep and dreamed again. I was driving down the road. Suzette was in the back seat and Todd Morris was in the front. We were helping Todd and Lori move furniture. I sometimes spontaneously sing different songs out of the blue. Suddenly, I began singing:

> *"This could be the last time, this could be the last time, maybe the last time, I don't know. Oh no ..."*

All three of us were pulled out of the car toward the sky, raptured toward heaven.

I awoke, and felt the shocked sensation as never before. The intensity of the "electrified" feeling was almost overwhelming. I looked at the clock. 4:30 a.m.

My nerves tingled. I was so shocked I could barely breathe. An overpowering sense of urgency filled me, enough that tears welled up in my eyes.

The last two dreams had not been nearly as intense; in fact, I thought I was simply getting used to the feeling. As I lay in bed, every nerve ending was on fire.

"God, I know this is from you," I prayed. "Open my eyes so I will know what to do with the dreams. I know you want me to share, but let me know what it really means, what you want me to tell."

I arose early. I couldn't go back to sleep. Chill bumps ran up my spine. Tears came to my eyes again. The sense of urgency had never felt as strong.

Is this the last time? Is time running out for our world? The intensity told me that it could happen at any time. The kingdom of God is at hand.

I looked up "astronomy" on the Internet and again came across the information concerning the Hale-Bopp comet. On November 14, 1996, Chuck Shramek of Houston took a CCD photograph of the comet and a nearby mysterious object. The unidentified object looked like the planet Saturn and, in Shramek's mind, followed Comet Hale-Bopp for more than one hour. (See photo at www.halebopp.com.)

Some people thought it may be a star behind the comet that was magnified by the gases trailing it. Some of the more interesting Internet copy tied it to the prophecies of Nostradamas, a sixteenth-century French physician and astrologer. Quatrain VI-97 of his writings says:

> At 5° by 40°, the sky will burn
> Fire is approaching the big new city
> A huge explosion will occur
> When some proof will be required concerning the Normans.

Personally, I don't know the significance of the comet, although it may be some additional astrological signs that season of the Return is here. I'm not in the business of making predictions and won't do so because it may take away from God's message. It would only be my prediction, not that of God. But some Bible passages are possibly involved:

> I will show wonders in the heavens...
> Joel 2:30 (NIV)

> For as lightning that comes from the east is visible even in the west, so will be the coming of the Son of Man. Matthew 24:27 (NIV)

Dan Lane had an interesting observation about the astrological factor.

> "The Bible talks about wonders in the heavens. Well, there has never been such a sight as that comet hitting Jupiter in 1994. Red moons. Now, three comets have recently been seen in the sky. It kinda makes you wonder."

My personal belief is that things are clicking into place, even among the stars and the heavens. This may be the last time.

But there's still a chance to change your mind.

Chapter 11

REVELATIONS

The edge was back. I began sharing the dreams with even more people. Bruce Parker and I were inducted into the Gideons International on Sunday morning of February 23. I shared it with them. I wanted to call Joe Senn about it, but due to the early hour, had waited. To my surprise, Joe was at the Gideons' meeting. He shared about the miraculous revivals breaking out around the area. I also shared about the dreams. Joe made this observation:

"Some of the revivals of old began with different people. In the early 1900s, it began with businessmen. They were closing down their shops and plants and having prayer meetings. The movement afoot now seems to center around young people — teenagers and young people under thirty-five or so."

The Gideons present were blessed by the testimonies. Exciting things are happening. It's a great time to be a Christian. I also shared about the dreams with my Sunday school class. Interestingly enough, our lesson was out of Matthew, chapter 25, concerning the Last Judgment. After I had finished, Tim Morris observed:

"This sounds like a Stephen King novel."

"Sound like?" I said. "Hey, I've been living it for the past six months."

Tuesday, February 25, 1997, was an extremely significant day. I shared the dreams with everyone in our law firm's Monroe office. Again, they expressed how blessed they were by the sharing of it. Marcus Murphy called me at lunch. We discussed the latest dream.

"Marcus, I really feel that something is going to happen soon. Of course, I don't know when, but it just feels like Jesus's return is about to happen. Whether it's two months or 2,000 years, who knows."

"Mary Ann and I were talking about the same thing the other night," he said. "You've probably read about this sheep cloning thing. Pretty soon scientists will be cloning man. We're becoming like God. How long can He permit this to continue?"

Later that day I was also called by Bruce Parker. He told me about a preacher named Mahaney. The guy had been a Hell's Angel type, riding motorbikes, etc. He said that God had audibly spoken to him four times, once to call him to the ministry. The second time, Bruce couldn't remember what had happened. Another time Mahaney heard the voice say, "Today you will need my strength" before learning of his brother's suicide.

"Two weeks ago he said God spoke to him for the fourth time and said, **'Tell my children I'm coming soon'**."

As Bruce and I talked, we discussed all of the fantastic things occurring.

"I need to share it with others," he said. "Even if it doesn't affect them now, it may later."

"What do you mean?"

"Well, if the true believers are raptured out, most of the people on earth will still be left behind. Maybe they'll understand once we're gone."

It was if a light went on in my head. I had been writing this manuscript, but not really knowing why. I hadn't thought about the people left behind. People would be searching for an explanation.

The question of whether the Church, the body of believers, will be taken out prior to the last Tribulation is one of the most hotly debated areas of "End Time" prophecy. My dreams haven't given me a clear answer. On one hand, the circumstances when I have been lifted up have been extremely ordinary, unexpected. Raking leaves, walking out of Sunday school, walking down the street, driving down the road. Yet are the visions literal or symbolic? Personally, I have always felt that God doesn't take us out of difficult circumstances, but gives us the strength to overcome them. The more I thought about it, the more I realized that the dreams weren't meant to answer any questions like these, but to simply stress one urgent message that Christ is returning soon.

"Maybe God is speaking to me through you, Bruce. Maybe that's what I'm supposed to do. To speak the truth concerning these things that are coming to pass. To show it to others by writing this book. Just suppose we are raptured out very soon. I don't know if that's the way it will happen or not, but suppose it does. How would the world explain it?"

"I don't know."

"Satan wouldn't sit idly by. He'd use every trick to

explain it away. The Big Lie. We're being saturated on TV and the movies with alien abductions on shows like the 'X-Files' and 'Independence Day.' Maybe the government will reveal that the Roswell incident actually occurred to calm everybody down or to unite the world under one leader to fend off the threat. Or maybe they'd use some cosmic event to explain the disappearance. Anything but the truth that Jesus had pulled away the believers."

It was a revelation, as if the entire purpose of my life had suddenly been revealed in a single instant. I had to share this message of Christ's return with others—by word, both written and spoken. I wasn't being "called" to preach. On the contrary, being a preacher would almost take away from the message that had been shown to an ordinary guy like me. But He did want me to share what He had revealed to me.

"Bruce, I haven't told anyone this. Ever since I was a little boy, I always knew that something great was going to happen to me. I'm not bragging. Maybe that explains the positive attitude I've always had. But I've always known. I didn't know if I'd be the governor or maybe president. But I did know that God had something great in store for me. I believe that this is it."

The season of God's return is upon us. The lightning is flashing in the east, and we can see it in the west. No one but the Father knows the date and hour, but we'll know the season. It is here. I felt it to the core of my being.

"I had prayed Sunday morning for God to open my eyes, to reveal what this is all about. Now I think I know."

I don't know the exact meaning of the dreams. But at least I know the message. The season of His return is at hand. The signs in the heavens reveal it, the visions of people like me show it, and the incredible outpouring of His Spirit illuminates it.

Are you ready?

Is your family?

What about your friends?

Chapter 12

SPIRITUAL WARFARE

The Marines are looking for a few good men. So is God.

But who is a good soldier?

The one who obeys. The one who does what he is told. The one who's been stripped of his old ways of thinking and listens only to the instructions of his commander. I would soon learn some valuable lessons in becoming a Spiritual Warrior.

On March 8, 1997, I awoke in the middle of the night. Unable to go back to sleep, I prayed. Confession had been the theme of that week's lesson at our Bible study group taught by Diana Lee, *Disciple's Prayer Life* by T. W. Hunt. My confession began with small things, but I eventually asked forgiveness for some the deepest and darkest secrets of my life, including broken promises to God.

"Take away the dirt and the guilt. Clean me."

I ended by quoting the Lord's Prayer:

> "... Your kingdom come, Your will be done, on earth as it is in heaven ..." Matthew 6:10 (NIV)

As I prayed these words, suddenly the electrified feeling coursed through me. I could barely move, my body almost numb, tingling. I felt clean. Pure. Full of the Holy Spirit.

After this experience, I realized the importance of bringing our dirty laundry to God. He's an expert cleaner, specializing in making even the most dingy people white as snow. It doesn't matter the nature of the sin. He can clean us.

> If we confess our sins, He is faithful and just and will forgive us our sins and to cleanse us from all unrighteousness. 1 John 1:9 (NKJV)

God wants a clean vessel into which he can pour Himself. We can become clean and filled with God by confession. It is a vital step in becoming a Spiritual Warrior.

Another important lesson concerned the nature of the battle. Know your enemy. That's a simple but profound instruction in the art of war. But who exactly are we fighting?

On March 9, 1997, I had another dream. I walked inside a very old cathedral-like building. A gothic church. The interior was dark and very creepy. The walls were of rock, wet and damp, and in the back of the church was a cave. Joe Senn, our church's staff evangelist, was surrounded by several other men. I was part of this group. Joe reminded me of General Patton, rallying the troops to fight. We were going into the cave to cast out demons.

As we neared the entrance, green shapes poured out of the mouth of the cave. One came towards me. It looked almost like the slime monster from the "Ghostbusters" movie, spectre-like and greenish, only this was not a friendly-looking ghost. It was wicked, evil. Horrible. As the demon neared me, I drew back my arm and opened my fist to deliver a blow to the forehead of the demon with the hard portion of my palm. I drove my hand into the thing's head, but it went right through the beast. The demon had no physical substance. An apparition.

I awoke with my heart racing. No electrified feeling, just the terror of a nightmare.

"You can't fight it physically; you must fight it spiritually. It's a spiritual battle."

These words raced through my mind as I woke up.

The next day I called Joe, not knowing if the dream had any special significance to him.

"My first question is, were we winning the battle?" he laughed.

"You were whaling away at them," I said with a smile. "Does it mean anything to you?"

"It sure does. For about the last five years, I've been engaged in spiritual warfare. A lot of people don't know that's part of my ministry. It's not something I go around telling everyone because it's so easily misunderstood."

Spiritual warfare. It wasn't a new concept to me. A few years ago, I had read a book by Frank Peretti called *This Present Darkness*. It detailed battles of angels and demons, an unseen fight that's occurring right around us.

The concept of demons is almost foreign today, except for movies like "The Exorcist." We think that stories about demons are "old wive's tales" based on misconceptions of mental illnesses and other diseases. However, a large part of Jesus' ministry consisted of casting out demons. Is this something that has relevance today?

A vivid example of spiritual warfare can be seen in my own family tree. My great-grandfather, Richard Moreland Doughty, had been an outlaw, a tough and rowdy fellow. He was an interesting guy. As a young man, he was ambushed at a baseball game and shot out of a hayloft. The bullet was lodged so close to his heart that the doctors couldn't remove it. Later, after he became a preacher and surgical techniques improved, the bullet was removed. Richard had reconciled with the fellow who had shot him. He handed the bullet to the man and said, jokingly, "Reload it and see if you can do a better job of it."

He was called to preach as a Southern Baptist pastor shortly after the birth of my grandfather, Alvin Oliver Doughty, Sr. Upon arriving home, he told his wife, "Mary Jane, God is calling me to preach. But I've got to go to town and whip Charlie Tullos just one more time." In Nebo, Louisiana, he was pastoring a Baptist church there. Often he would go across the road and into the woods to pray. He knelt by a small sweetgum tree and would cut a slash on it with his knife when had finished. Now it's a towering tree with many scars on it, much like a healed appendix wound. People in the area call it "The Prayer Tree."

My great-grandfather was a powerful preacher and man of God, but five of his six sons became alcoholics. Satan couldn't get him, so he wreaked havoc among his children. The "demon" of alcoholism has raged within our family ever since. Donald Doughty, one of my father's cousins, is the son of the only non-alcoholic of the group. He is a Baptist preacher, too.

It's as if there is a visible struggle between good and evil, God and Satan, even within my own family. I spoke about these things with my father.

"David, the devil doesn't want the Doughtys to be working for the Lord," Daddy said. "God has gifted our family with the ability to influence others. The devil doesn't want that to happen."

Spiritual warfare is a battle for souls, the ultimate battle because our souls are the only eternal possession we have. But there are only two sides. There is no "in between." No middle ground. Jesus said it quite clearly:

> He who is not with me is against me, and he who does not gather with me scatters. Luke 11:23 (NIV)

Are you gathering or scattering?

This dream brought home to me a frightening truth: The presence of evil in our world today is real, just as real as God's presence. Our enemy isn't each other, but something quite different. You can't fight the battle physically—it's a spiritual war. We need to become strong in the spiritual sense. Just as a person exercises to build muscles, we need to exercise and grow spiritually to become warriors of God.

> Finally, my brethren, be strong in the Lord and in the power of His might. Put on the whole armor of God, that you may be able to stand against the wiles of the devil. For we do not wrestle against flesh and blood, but against principalities, against powers, against the rulers of the darkness of this age, against spiritual hosts of wickedness in the heavenly places. Therefore take up the whole armor of God, that you may be able

to withstand in the evil day, and having done all, to stand. Stand therefore, having girded your waist with truth, having put on the breastplate of righteousness, and having shod your feet with the preparation of the gospel of peace; above all, taking the shield of faith with which you will be able to quench all the fiery darts of the wicked one. And take the helmet of salvation, and the sword of the Spirit, which is the word of God. Ephesians 6:10-17 (NKJV)

Another important aspect of the March 9th dream was that the demons were actually within the church. This theme of evil in the church was also experienced in a dream by Tom Allen. On a rainy, dreary Sunday in March of 1997, Tom Allen was taking a hot bath. He had been extremely busy, preparing for his first jury trial. He sat there, reflecting on some of the depressing things that had been happening, perhaps a reflection of the dreariness outside. Tom's uncle had recently died of cancer, and his aunt and cousins had been huddled together at the gravesite in similar cold, rainy conditions. Also, he had found five puppies under a nearby house. The mother was a big, ugly dog, part mutt and part Catahoula Cur. It's a mean dog, believed to have killed sheep in the Oak Ridge area. One of the puppies had been hit by a car. The puppy with the weird eyes. The dog's eyes were half brown, half blue. Tom had called Chris Morris, a local veterinarian, over to see if he could help the puppy. They couldn't get to it, and Tom was barely able to reach one of its legs. He pulled it out by a leg that had been crushed. The dog howled in a pitch, not simply of pain, but a mournful cry of utter sorrow.

As Tom sat in the tub and thought about the howl, it triggered the memory of a dream he had while in law school. The dream was so buried in his subconscious that he would have never thought of it had it not been for the cry of the little puppy.

In the dream, Tom walked up to a huge Catholic church to visit his aunt and cousins. They were living in this church, although it was in a state of great disrepair. He stepped inside and saw his aunt and cousins. They were incredibly sad. His uncle was not there. The foyer of the church had a long hall with smaller "Sunday school" type rooms to either side. It was very dark, and the only light was coming from one of the small rooms where they were living. Trash littered the marble floor. Tom had the feeling that his aunt and cousins were embarrassed and sad to be there. At the rear, a set of large doors opened up into the sanctuary. As Tom neared them, he felt afraid. He opened the doors and the room was even darker inside. He saw a movement in the rear. A huge, mongrel dog of a motley, grayish hue was sitting up front. The dog was angular and large, almost non-descript.

"Is that your dog?" Tom asked his aunt and cousins.

"No, that's not our dog!" they said nervously.

The dog was eating out of the communion dish, a gold plate with an inscription around the lip. The hair rose on the back of Tom's neck.

The dog looked up at him, bared its fangs, growling. Its eyes glowed in a fluorescent color as if it were possessed. As the dog glared at him with his evil eyes, Tom woke up.

His heart racing, Tom was relieved that it was only a dream. He was home for the Christmas holidays and described it as a still, wintery night. He lay in bed trying to gather his wits about himself, when a dog's howl erupted underneath his window. The sound jolted him out of bed. He couldn't see a dog out of his window.

"That howl was the exact kind of mournful sound made by the little puppy when I pulled him out. Somehow that triggered my memory," Tom said.

"Is there something going on in churches? Some type of evil presence?" I asked. "These dreams are too similar. Yours of a demon dog eating out of a communion dish. Mine of casting demons out of a cave in the rear of a church-like building. What's going on?"

Beware. There are certainly wolves in our midst, hiding in sheep's clothing. You don't need to believe what anyone says simply because he or she is a preacher, priest or reverend. You need to compare what is said with the Scriptures, with the Word of God. That also goes for anything you read in this book or any "spiritual" experience you have. Ask the question: "Is this biblical?"

The Word of God is vital to defeat evil. Jesus Christ faced temptation by Satan in the desert and fended off each attempt by quoting Scripture. We need to arm ourselves with God's Word. Study it, memorize it, live with it. Take a stand.

A battle is raging around us.

Chapter 13

THE WIND BLOWS

> "As they were walking along and talking together, suddenly a chariot of fire and horses of fire appeared and separated the two of them, and Elijah went up to heaven in a whirlwind." 2 Kings 2:11 (NIV)

On April 2, 1997, I visited Ron Morien, a local pastor of the Rayville Assembly of God Church. Ron is a bright, energetic man with a quick smile and true love for God. He had been very active in the Richland Parish Promise Keepers group. I dropped off a copy of the manuscript and shared with him about the dreams.

"David," he told me, " I'm not one of these pastors who constantly has a new revelation from God. But I've got to tell you. About thirty days ago, I had a dream or vision. The only one I've ever had. I had awakened on a Sunday morning about 6:00 a.m. I normally go to church early and pray. As I was lying in bed half asleep, I was suddenly in the foyer of our church. It has large glass doors at the entrance. Sometimes I will look out of the windows at the Rayville Water Tower, praying for our town. Outside, the sky was dark, the wind blowing. I saw a tornado coming directly towards the church. 'It's going to hit us,' I thought. The tornado came closer to the church until it suddenly sucked the glass doors right off their hinges. The doors tumbled away into it. Despite the tremendous winds, nothing in the foyer was disturbed. Not me, not even the morning programs.

"I felt like God was telling me that He was going to blow the doors off the churches in these last days. Not just Assemblies of God, but all churches. I preached this vision to my church. Believe me, we had **church** that day."

Tornadoes. Ron wasn't the first person to describe a spiritual vision or dream concerning a whirlwind. When I got back to the office I told Tom Allen about it.

"I've had a recurring dream for a long time about a tornado," Tom said.

"You're kidding me."

He shook his head.

"The most vivid dream is one I had years ago. We were riding in a Bronco, heading towards Oak Ridge. The driver was Lynn Wiggins, one of the few Catholics in Oak Ridge. As she was driving, in the rearview mirror, I could see a tornado. It was beautiful, silvery, flashing, and glittering. We debated whether to outrun it or stop and let it consume us. It wasn't as if we were scared to death of it."

On April 26, 1997, I also had a dream in the "tornado" category. I was running in a race, the course meandering along a series of blacktop roads through the countryside. I've loved to run for quite some time. In high school I ran sprint relays on the track team, but hated distance running. However, during my first years of law school, I learned to love it. A three or four mile run was just what the doctor ordered to relieve the intense stress.

The race was long, and I was perspiring greatly. I also noticed that I was wearing an ill-fitting pair of Hush Puppies rather than running shoes. I saw a spectacular sunset of crimsons, oranges, yellow, and pinks. As I ran and studied the glorious sight, I suddenly saw a tremendous tornado moving toward me. It split into twin tornadoes, writhing and twisting like snakes. Some of the other runners and I took shelter in an abandoned house. We lay in the hall, still mesmerized by the twin tornadoes framed by the doorway. As it grew nearer and nearer, I woke up.

I believe the dreams of tornadoes symbolize the blowing of the Holy Spirit upon our land and our churches. God is pouring out His Spirit on us. Many of the pastors and older Christians in our area have commented that they've never seen anything like what's going on in churches now. The awesome power of God is like a tornado and He is sending that power our way. That's good news for those who recognize Him, but for those who don't know Him, it will mean destruction.

> The LORD has His way
> In the whirlwind and in the storm,
> And the clouds are the dust of His feet.
>
> Nahum 1:3 (NKJV)

> See, the storm of the LORD
> will burst out in wrath,
> a whirlwind swirling down
> on the heads of the wicked.
>
> Jeremiah 23:19 (NIV)

There is indeed a wind blowing through churches, ripping off the doors. Churches around the world are changing, becoming energized. Ron Morien had told me of the Brownsville Assembly of God Church in Pensacola, Florida. A revival had begun on Father's Day, June 18, 1995, sparked by a wind blowing through the congregation, and continues even today. Over 100,000 people of all walks of life and denominations have been saved.

> When the day of Pentecost came, they were all together in one place. Suddenly, a sound like the blowing of a violent wind came from heaven and filled the whole house where they were sitting.
>
> Act. 2:1-2 (NIV)

During this time, I continued to pray concerning God's direction about these dreams and visions. What did He want me to do with them?

A friend had opened her Bible at random one day and read the following verses. She pointed them out to me, thinking they may apply:

> Then the Lord answered me and said:
>
> Write the vision
> And make it plain on tablets,
> That he may run who reads it.
> For the vision is yet for an appointed time;
> But at the end it will speak, and it will not lie.
> Though it tarries, wait for it;
> Because it will surely come,
> It will not tarry.
>
> Habakkuk 2:2-3 (NKJV)

After reading these verses, I knew that God wanted me to write down my dreams, but He also wanted me to get the written word out. I felt like a herald, a messenger of the appointed time.

I also prayed about the dreams. If God wanted me to know anything about the timing, I wanted to know. Not the day and hour, but the general nature of the "appointed time."

That evening, I awoke in the middle of the night. No dream, but the words of a song from my high school days were playing in my head:

Urgent, urgent, Emergency,
Urgent, urgent, Emergency,
Urgent, urgent, urgent, urgent ...

Chapter 14

RIPPLE EFFECTS

As a boy, my friends and I dropped rocks off a bridge into a muddy stream. The smooth surface of the water would be disturbed as ripple effects radiated from where the stone struck. The rings were small at first, but grew greater and greater in size.

Since the "Last Time" dream of February 23, I had shifted into high gear. God wanted me to get into action. I had finished a partial draft of this book and had a number of copies printed and bound at Kinkos. These books were given to family and friends around the country. I also began speaking to churches of various denominations. Little did I realize that I was dropping stones into the water.

Monty Hogg and I stood outside his house discussing the *Visions* manuscript.

"You'll never really know the ripple effects of what you've done," he said.

"It's not me, Monty. It's like the book has a life of its own. The Holy Spirit has been all over it. Even from the start. After I had spent a good deal of money to get the manuscript printed, I won $1000 at the Riverfield Day drawing. It's unreal."

Monty's mother and father had come across a copy of

Visions a few weeks earlier. They had been so moved by it that they shared it at their church in Delhi one Sunday night. Their pastor, Charles Kendrick, later told me that a young girl about eighteen had been in the congregation that night. After church, she approached him and told him that she wasn't "ready," but she wanted to get that way. She was saved that evening.

This wasn't an isolated event. Marcus Murphy, the pastor at First Baptist of Delhi, called me one day, the excitement in his voice barely contained.

"You're not going to believe this."

"Try me."

"Bud LaPrarie and I were painting at the church. He told me about something that happened at his business. He had a copy of your book there. When he went to lunch, he left it, one of his employees picked it up. She began reading it. When Bud returned, she was still going through it. He told her to finish. When she did, she was crying. She told Bud that she was a Christian, but that she and her husband had stopped going to church. She was going to make a change."

Marcus continued.

"We're going to print up one hundred copies of your book, if that's all right.

"We're going to use it as an outreach tool for some of our church members that have become inactive."

One of the most dramatic ripple effects has been the opened door for others to share about their experiences. After baring my soul for all to see, other people have felt comfortable telling me things that they haven't told anyone else. This has happened so many times that I now believe that experiences like mine are **more common** than not.

Johnny and Jan Morris are close friends. Johnny's a soft-spoken, down-to-earth farmer, and not one you'd expect to have this type of experience. But then again, neither am I. Johnny had read *Visions* with great excitement. He called me the next day.

"I had a dream not long ago about Kathy."

Kathy was Kathy Mills Wilkerson, Johnny's cousin who had been killed in a car accident in May of 1996. Kathy's death had been a real tragedy in our community. She left behind three young children. Her mother, Mrs. Virginia Mills, had struggled in dealing with Kathy's death and at the same time, in raising three young kids.

"She told me not to worry about her," he continued. "She was in a much better place. She said to take care of the kids. It was just as real as the two of us talking now. I told Jan, but no one else. The next day, we were in the grocery store and guess who we saw. Aunt Virginia. I didn't say anything. Then I went to the meat department and guess who again? Aunt Virginia. She began to pour out her heart to me. I felt like I needed to tell her about the dreams, so I did. Both of us were standing there in the grocery store crying our eyes out".

"The strange thing is that LuAnn Wisenor Young had a dream about Kathy the exact same night as I did. Three clouds had come toward her in a dream, and she saw Kathy. Kathy told her that she couldn't tell her everything now, but that everything was going to be fine. She told LuAnn about the same things she had told me. LuAnn shared this with Aunt Virginia the next day."

The power of his words brought tears to my eyes. What a wonderful God we have! He cares, He listens, He loves. Enough to give a heartbroken mother some reassurances about her daughter. Often He uses dreams in this manner to help us when we're struggling. Mechelle Terral's story illustrates this well.

On April 25, 1997, I received a phone call at my law office.

"David, this is Mechelle Terral from Delhi. You don't know me, but I just finished your book, and I had to talk to you."

Mechelle is a mother of three boys, ages six, four, and twenty-one months. Most of her days are spent chasing them around the house. Both she and her husband Brad want her to be home with the boys, but on occasion she feels "like a mama". No uniqueness, no special talents.

Several years ago, she and Brad had lived in Dallas. At the time, Mechelle was at home with her first two boys. Most of her friends worked and had no children. She felt strangely out of place. In an effort to be productive, she wrote and illustrated a children's book about her oldest son Bo. For over one year, she did nothing with it until one day she felt an urging . She thought God was prompting her to get it published. She sent it to a Christian publisher in Dallas. Five weeks later, the rejection letter arrived in the mail. Mechelle was angry with God, as though He had abandoned her. She felt empty, as if her life was worthless, meaningless.

That night, she was still upset when she went to bed. When she finally went to sleep, Mechelle dreamed about taking care of Bo and Hunter and how important they were.

Upon waking, she heard a distinct and profound voice:

"You are the ark of my covenant."

She awoke with a start, but was relieved...the anxiety gone. She was excited, calm, relieved, happy, and confused all at one time. She knew God was telling her something, but what?

She searched her Bible for an answer and found that he Ark of the Covenant was the gold-overlaid box holding the Ten Commandments. When Brad arrived home, she asked him about it. He had always been able to explain biblical things to her.

"Mechelle, God loves you and our children. He thinks our children are important, no matter what this world thinks about mothers who are at home. He thinks it's the most important thing you can do—raise your children to know and love Him. You're like an ark—you believe in Jesus Christ so you hold God's covenant. He's assuring you. You're doing His will."

Afterwards, Mechelle felt incredibly close to God. Her prayers were being answered. It was as if He heard everything she said.

"Last night, I read part of your book before I had to put it down so I could get my three kids to bed," Mechelle continued. "My heart was heavy and I prayed that I would be more of an ambassador for God. I also prayed for my son

Hunter who has had a lot of trouble with his kidneys and may require surgery. That night I dreamed I was holding Hunter's hand. We were outside and looking for Brad and the rest of our family. I was tired and wanted to sleep, but I couldn't rest until I was next to him. People were around, and I searched faces for someone to help me find Brad. I saw my sister who had recently been saved. I didn't say anything to her, but felt comforted. I also saw my other sister who I have been spiritually concerned about. She looked at me and said, 'I don't know.'

"I kept searching and eventually found Brad. My other two boys were with him. We found a place to rest and lay down. A church was to my left. It was made of dark brick, surrounded by trees, and we appeared to be in a community setting. We stopped, and I fell asleep, although I had difficulty because I wasn't close enough to Brad. When I woke up, I was again holding Hunter's hand. I saw another church begin to appear across from me. It wasn't an ordinary church, but looked like a Roman type of building. It was made of stone or marble with white columns and steps. Above it was a bright cloud that lit up the church. The building was so bright white that it was almost yellow. The church building started crumbling, caving in. A cloud of dust from its destruction rose to meet the cloud, and it formed a single bright column.

"I saw people walking out of the building unharmed, unhurt. They weren't looking back, but were acting as if nothing had happened. Hunter and I kept walking toward the church. I wasn't scared to go near it, even though it was falling apart. As I approached, I noticed that people were going up in the bright cloud column. Then Hunter and I began to rise.

`We're going to see Jesus,' I heard someone say.

`We're going to see Jesus!' I said to Hunter.

`Mama, we're going to see Jesus!' Hunter said.

"We rose in the air, but I felt a tugging at my feet.

"`Let me go! Let me go,' I thought. We began to shoot upwards. I felt like Hunter wasn't close enough. I wanted to make sure I wasn't going to drop him. As I pulled him closer, it felt like I was doing a flip. Then I knew it was okay—holding his hand was enough. He didn't have to be right next to me. Suddenly we were instantly in the brightest light I've ever seen. I felt total comfort. Then I woke up. My body was tingling, my heart racing. I was shaking.

"I woke Brad up and talked to him about the dream. I felt God was telling me several things. I was afraid to let Hunter leave my side, but God was telling me that he'd be fine. Also, the church was crumbling, but I wasn't scared of it. It's the safe place to be. That's where we connect to God. But the strongest impression I got from the dream was about family. I wanted mine with me. I think God wants us to get our families together. To focus on Him as a family. Get ready for Him. I've realized that both of the dreams revealed the most important thing to God—our families. Raising godly children. A family that thrives on Him."

Later, I told my brother Terry and Johnny B. Hoychick about Mechelle's dreams.

"The church is going to be no more after the Rapture," Johnny B. said. "It's going to be taken out. That's what the crumbling church could mean. And the people leaving it could be those who go to church but aren't true believers. Kinda like Terry," he joked at my brother. We all laughed.

As I began to disseminate the book, I felt as though I needed to give a copy to the local rabbi. It wasn't a compulsion to try to convert him to Christianity, but I thought it was important for him to have one. I called and made an appointment at the Temple B'Nai Israel in Monroe. I met the rabbi and discussed the dreams with him. He had some important observations.

"As an attorney, you know that you'll never be able to prove the dreams to anyone. But do you remember the movie *Oh God!* with George Burns? They kept trying to get tangible evidence of God. Photographs, recordings. None of it came out. You must remember that the most important proof you have is the change in your own life. That's something people can see. How you live your life is the evidence of God's touch."

The rabbi is right. Each of our lives should demonstrate God's love and His presence. As I look back, I know that I'm no longer the same guy I was before the dreams began. Perhaps others can see it. I hope they can. Maybe that's what it means to "let our light shine before men."

> In the same way, let your light shine before men, that they may see your good deeds and praise your Father in heaven.
>
> Matthew 5:16 (NIV)

One of the most dramatic ripple effects occurred on April 27, 1997, the morning after my tornado dream. On the fourth Sunday of each month, the Gideons in our area meet at the Saljobar in Delhi for breakfast and then go to different juvenile prisons facilities in Tallulah, Louisiana. Rayland Trisler and Wayne McManus had invited me to speak. It was a dark and rainy day, so rainy, in fact, that the facility where I was scheduled to speak had to cancel the meeting. Instead, we went to Christian Acres, a holding facility for approximately sixty to seventy boys from the ages of ten to sixteen. These aren't boys who have simply painted graffiti on a wall. Most are hardened criminals before they can even be placed there.

We gathered at the gym that morning, the rain almost deafening in the metal building. Rayland had come with me, as had Milton Day and "Big" John Pritchett.

I stood at mid-court in front of the boys.

"I'm not here to preach to you today. But I'm going to tell you the story of what's happened to me. It'll probably be one of the strangest you've ever heard..."

When I had finished, I was unsure of the response of the boys. Milton began speaking to them. He speaks often at prisons. Milton is a dear man with an unquenchable hunger to share the gospel with those behind bars. He has good reason for it. He was in jail for most of his young adult life, a hardened and unrepentant criminal, until the day he met the Lord Jesus face to face. He's been changed ever since.

"He that has an ear, let him hear," Milton told them. The boys needed to listen and answer the call of Jesus.

"Should we give an invitation?" I asked Big John after Milton had finished.

"Do whatever the Lord leads you to do," he said.

Rayland and I went to mid-court again. I asked those who had never accepted Christ as their Savior to come forward as everyone else prayed.

Soon one boy came.

Then another.

Then two more.

It was amazing what the Holy Spirit was doing. By the time we had finished, eighteen boys had accepted Christ, almost one-third of the group present. We had witnessed a true miracle of God. The wind was blowing.

On the trip home, Rayland and I were discussing the events.

"What if I'd never shared with anyone about the dreams. Just think of the blessings I'd have missed. Like what we saw today."

Then it hit me.

Our entire lives are like those rocks I dropped into the stream as a boy. Almost every act we take sends out ripple effects. Some for the good, some for the bad. How many times had anger, harsh words, gossip or hatred radiated out of my actions? It sickened me to think about it. The things we do have impact on others. We reap what we sow. Before you drop a rock, think about its effect. Make sure it's the right one to drop. And if you drop rocks for God, He'll bless you in ways you've never dreamed.

Chapter 15

Two-Minute Warning

Football has been my favorite sport since childhood. I grew up with memories of the Dallas Cowboys and my hero Roger Staubach. During the 1970s there wasn't a better quarterback in the last two minutes of a ballgame than Roger the Dodger. I'll never forget the "Hail Mary" pass. As time expired, Staubach launched a bomb to Drew Pearson, a miracle pass to beat the Minnesota Vikings in the playoffs. My brother Terry, a diehard Viking's fan, won't forget it either.

Another of my favorite games occurred in the 1980s while I was home from Tech, watching a ballgame on a Friday afternoon. Doug Flutie was quarterbacking Boston College versus Bernie Kosar and the Miami Hurricanes. I was only able to catch the end of the game, but it had more action in the last two minutes than most have in sixty minutes. It ended with Flutie throwing a last-second bomb to a receiver in the end zone to win the game.

The term "two-minute warning" has even deeper significance to me after a dream I had on May 12, 1997. In the dream, I was leading three horses by the reins. The nearest one was black. I can't remember the color of the other two. I was leading the horses to the barn at Daddy Ford and Mama Pearl's house. My grandparents lived near me in the country during my childhood, and they always had horses and other livestock.

I opened the gate and let the horse go inside the fenced corral area. While I got some feed for them, I prayed to myself. It wasn't anything fancy, just a simple word of thanks to God. I took the feed to the trough and poured it in. Suddenly, I heard a voice. Not a deep thundering voice, but one quiet and distinct.

"YOU WANT A WARNING ... TWO-MINUTE WARNING."

I saw the words "Two-Minute Warning" flash before my eyes.

What happened next almost defies description.

A force, almost like a bolt of energy, blasted into me from above. I saw tentacles of energy before closing my eyes. It was if I had been struck by lightning.

From the impact of the force, I was pressed down into the bed mattress. I tried to scream but was paralyzed. I couldn't move. I could only scream with my mind.

"No ...!"

There wasn't any pain, but I knew I couldn't handle the force or energy for very long. Finally, it subsided, and I woke up.

My nerve endings were tingling, the electrified sensation was the most intense it had ever been. My heart was racing. The first thought in my mind was how insignificant I was. I was nothing, an insect in comparison to that power. Another major impression from the dream was "fear of God." The fear of the Lord is a message that isn't preached much in most churches any more, and if it is, it's watered down as just a "healthy awe or respect" for God.

After experiencing just a drop of God's power, I realized that we need to FEAR GOD. If we truly realized who God is, we wouldn't be doing a lot of the things we do.

I was so frightened that I woke up Suzette.

"I just had another dream," I said. "It scared me to death."

I pulled her close to me.

"You've got to hold me."

"You've been reading too many of those books," she said.

"Yeah, you're right. I **have** been reading a lot of prophetic books, but that's just it. I haven't been dreaming every night."

When I finally got up the courage, I looked at the alarm clock. 2:30 a.m. I was still too scared to go to the bathroom by myself.

I prayed for God to open my mind and reveal to me what He wanted me to know. As I lay there, unable to go back to sleep, I suddenly saw patterns of light swirling over me.

"I'm really going crazy now," I thought to myself.

I even closed my eyelids and could see what appeared to be almost "wings" of light.

Was it a host of angels flying around me?

I can't say for sure; the forms were indistinct, but that's certainly the impression I had. As I watched in fascination, I suddenly had the "raptured" feeling again, my body tingling, my heart racing.

"Whew! This is too much to take," I thought.

In the morning when I got up to go to work, I was weak. My knees were watery, without strength, as if I'd been sick all night.

As I ate breakfast, I thought about the dream.

Horses. The horses were significant. My first thought was of the four horses of the Apocalypse. Revelation, chapter six talks about the breaking of the seals. The first seal releases the White Horse of the Conqueror. The second releases the Red Horse of War. The third seal releases the Black Horse of Famine. I had been leading three horses. One had been black. What did it mean—leading and feeding the horse of Famine?

The same chapter in Revelation ends with the breaking of the sixth seal. A great earthquake occurs. The sun turns black, and the moon to blood.

As I drove to work, I stopped at the grocery store to pick up the *USA Today*. The headlines of the May 12, 1997, issue startled me:

(1) An earthquake had occurred in Iran, registering 7.1 on the Richter scale, killing an estimated 2400 people near Qaen.

(2) IBM's Deep Blue Computer defeated Gary Kasparov, reigning world chess champion. Computer had triumphed over man.

(3) United States Secretary of State Madelyn Albright "sees her own path to the Middle East."

The way the paper was folded, showing only Albright's eyes, was especially disturbing. The night before, I had gone into the grocery store to get some dog food. On the spur of the moment, I bought a "*Sun*" tabloid that told about the Dead Sea Scroll prophecies. According to this very "reliable" source, a Dead Sea scroll scholar claimed that prophecies contained in the documents revealed that a well-known international woman would unwittingly bring about war in the Middle East. On the cover of the May 13, 1997 *Sun*, a pair of female eyes stared from a mushroom cloud. It was the thinly-veiled eyes of Hilary Clinton. However, the eyes on the Sun reminded me of Albright's on the *USA Today* cover.

I was still greatly troubled when I arrived at the office. I told Terry and Johnny about the dream.

"I'm reminded of something Susan always tells me when I'm watching a game on TV," Johnny said. "She'll ask, 'Why are you watching that game? Nothing ever happens until the last two minutes anyway'."

Tom Allen had also arrived at the office, and told me about a dream he had the same night.

"I dreamed I was at Tiger Stadium to watch a LSU football game. I was in a box that was supposed to have a good view, but I couldn't see the field. Then I heard over the

PA system that you were representing LSU to call the coin toss. I was like 'Allright! David always wins the coin toss!' They tossed the coin. I heard you say 'Heads.' 'Heads it is,' the ref said. I went down to the field. I never saw you, but I could see the field. It was beautiful. More beautiful ... especially beautiful. The Tigers were in their white uniforms, the field was dark green."

Tom paused.

"I told Hannah about it this morning, but it didn't really mean anything until you told me about yours. The football connection is undeniable. Two-Minute Warning. Then I dream the same night that you're at a LSU football game."

Tom was right. It was more than coincidence.

Two minutes. What does it mean? How long are two minutes to God?

I don't know the answers, but I do know the impressions God had given me. The seconds are ticking off the clock. Both teams are intensifying their efforts. The game is almost over.

Chapter 16

ALL IN THE FAMILY

... Your sons and daughters will prophesy ...
Joel 2:28 (NIV)

When the visions began, little did I know that it would become a family thing. Terry's ten-year old son, Matt, began having dreams. He woke Terry and Annie one night, scared to death. He had dreamed about a flood. They live near Boeuf River. Matt saw wave after wave of water pouring out of the woods across from them. Water was rising, destroying things and people in its path. Matt watched someone drown in a flood, and he awoke, frightened by the horrible nightmare. Terry wouldn't realize the significance of it until later.

In May of 1997, Matt had another disturbing vision. He dreamed that he was outside, and the entire sky was dark as night. A terrible storm was raging. Matt knew it was the end of the world. Suddenly, he saw a bright, brownish cloud in the sky. Words were written on the cloud:

GOD
HIS SON
HIM

"What do you think it means, David?" he asked me one day.

"I don't know, Matt. What'd you think about it?"

"It made me feel like Jesus is coming again. And so is the end of the world."

Matt's dream were unknown to my sister Dana. Dana is the baby of our family and always will be, even though she's twenty-eight. She's also the beauty of the family as well, with a dark complexion, dark eyes and hair. She and her husband Jeff, recently had a new addition, Mary Margaret, born in October 1996. Dana's world had been preoccupied with motherhood. She wasn't expecting a call from God.

On successive nights, May 17 and 18, 1997, Dana had two incredible dreams. The first was strikingly similar to Matt's. Jeff, Mary Margaret, and she were in New Orleans near the Mississippi River. Across from the river was a grove of very tall, pine trees. Dana saw a huge tidal wave rise from the trees, coming toward the city. Wave after wave poured out from the trees, flooding New Orleans. Everyone panicked, rushing madly through the streets. "There's no way out. It's coming too fast," people screamed.

As Jeff and Dana approached the middle of a drawbridge, suddenly a fellow panicked and pushed a button. The bridge began to fold upward. Dana and Mary Margaret were hanging from ropes on one side, while Jeff was hanging on the other side. Jeff kept his cool, encouraging Dana to be calm and climb upward. All this time, the water in the city was continuing to rise. Eventually, a rescue crew from helicopters, saved all three of them. At the moment they were safe inside the helicopter, the waters began to recede.

The next morning, a Sunday, Dana had another dream. She was inside a large warehouse-like building, with thousands of people grouped together in long lines. All adults, no children. It was a prison. Dana knew that

Christians were being burned alive, cremated in elevator shafts. A guard had sympathy for her and told Dana, Jeff, my brother Terry, and me to follow him to a "safe" shaft.

"You won't be destroyed inside these shafts. These will keep you from the fire."

Dana found it difficult to have faith in the guard and was afraid this was just another trick. The guard took us to another room. It was dark and filled with people. Dana recognized several high school friends. The guard led us into a shaft and instructed us to strap ourselves to the wall. As the guard shut the door, Dana couldn't help thinking, "Where are my family and friends? Why didn't I get them?"

The shaft began to drop very fast, plastering us to the wall. At the bottom, fire began springing up on the floor, but the men began to stomp it out. Dana heard shrill screams from outside the shaft. She could feel the pain of those dying.

Suddenly, the elevator shaft doors opened, and a figure was silouhetted in the frame. He looked at Dana. He was powerfully built and dressed in a dark, conservative pin-stripped suit and tie. His face was scarred, but distinguished. His hair was dark, his hairline receding. His left eye was bulging and "cock-eyed".

Dana instantly knew this man was the Beast.

The Antichrist.

He looked at us.

"Sh__! They're still alive," he said.

Despite his power, Dana knew he couldn't harm us anymore. As we were escaping out of a doorway, the Beast poured a clear liquid onto Jeff and Dana. The liquid seemed to eat through their clothes like acid.

Once outside, a black man saw the liquid. He was calm, but concerned. "What's that?" he asked.

"He poured it on us as we were coming out," Dana said.

"He's trying to destroy you," the black man said. "You may get sick."

Dana could feel his kindness and love, but knew the situation was very serious.

As we made our way out of the jail, Dana could see miles and miles of people imprisoned by the Beast. Most were calling out to us for help. Dana went up to a black man, grabbing his hand and holding it. All of us were ministering to these people behind the bars, most were skinny and emaciated. We moved throughout the area, helping and encouraging those locked inside.

Dana awoke, hearing a song ringing in her mind:

Go tell it on the mountain,
Over the hills and ev'rywhere;
Go tell it on the mountain,
Our Jesus Christ is born.

The dreams made a dramatic impact in Dana's life, setting her afire for God. She felt like she had been drifting away from God, but the dreams were the spark she needed to jump-start her spiritual life.

Matt and Dana's dreams of a tidal wave and flood could mean different things. Many times in the Bible, water is used to symbolize the Holy Spirit. Some people have suggested these dreams could mean that God is pouring out His Spirit on mankind now. Others see it as a sign of destruction just as it was in Noah's day.

However, Dana's vision of the Beast was really disturbing. Christians were being persecuted and cremated.

The Tribulation.

I've heard a saying. We should hope for the Rapture, but be prepared for the Tribulation. I don't know if the Beast will look like Dana's vision of him or whether it's symbolic, but we will know the Beast by his actions:

> He also forced everyone, small and great, rich and poor, free and slave, to receive a mark on his right hand or on his forehead, so that no one could buy or sell unless he had the mark, which is the name of the beast or the number of his name. This calls for wisdom. If anyone has insight, let him calculate the number of the beast, for it is man's number. His number is 666.
>
> Revelation 13: 16-18 (NIV)

We must remember the warning John heard from the third angel. Don't take the mark! It's not just the kiss of death. It's the kiss of hell.

> If anyone worships the beast and his image and receives his mark on the forehead or on the hand, he too, will drink of the wine of God's fury, which has been poured full strength into the cup of his wrath. He

> will be tormented with burning sulfur in the presence of the holy angels and of the Lamb. And the smoke of their torment rises for ever and ever. There is no rest day or night for those who worship the beast and his image, or for anyone who receives the mark of his name.
>
> Revelation 14:9-11 (NIV)

I don't know what the future holds for us. But if the darkness grows greater, and we must endure the Tribulation, we must remember that we can't lose faith.

Even if that faith costs us our life.

> Blessed are the dead who die in the Lord from now on. Revelation 14:13 (NIV)

Remember this truth. The Beast can only kill your flesh. He can't harm your soul.

Chapter 14

SIGNS, SIGNS, EVERYWHERE A SIGN

Before I began having these dreams, I never attempted to look for signs of the end times. I was no doomsday watcher. Now, it's as if my eyes have been opened to see things that are going around us. Or is it simply that my antenna is now attuned to such matters? You be the judge.

1. **Israel's Rebirth.**

> I myself will gather the remnant of my flock out of all countries where I have driven them and will bring them back to their pasture, where they will be fruitful and increase in number.
>
> Jeremiah 23:3 (NIV)

Perhaps the greatest sign in modern history occurred on May 14, 1948, when the nation of Israel was reborn. After the destruction of the temple in 70 A.D. by the Romans, Jews had been scattered from their promised land to all ends of the earth. It's remarkable that a nation which hadn't existed for almost 2,000 years came back into being. History has many examples of great nations that were destroyed. Once captured, the peoples would be intermixed with the victors, soon losing any racial, cultural or religious sense of identity. The melting pot of war. Think about it. Where are the Philistines now? Somehow, this didn't happen with the Jews. They retained their sense of nationality throughout ancient and modern history, even without a place to call home. Forty-nine years ago, a miracle happened when Israel once again became a country and the Jews once again had a place to call their own. Their Promised Land.

On that day the Lord made a covenant with Abraham and said,

> "To your descendants I give this land, from the river of Egypt to the great river, the Euphrates."
>
> Genesis 15:18 (NIV)

In Matthew, chapter 24, Jesus uses an analogy of the fig tree in discussing the end times. Many believe that Israel is referred to as the "fig tree," and it has now bloomed again. A sign of the Return.

Prophecy in the Bible is keyed to the nation of Israel. It is often referred to as "God's time clock." Keep a close eye on Israel, and more particularly Jerusalem.

In 1967, during the Six Day War, Israel regained its precious crown jewel. Jerusalem, the Holy City. Three of the major religions of the world look to this place with incredible fervor. To the Jew, it is a holy site of God's Temple, originally built by King Solomon. To the Christian, it is the site of Jesus' Crucifixion and Resurrection. To the Muslim, it is the place where Mohammed stepped into heaven.

Jerusalem is unlike any other city in the world. Because of this, it is unlikely Jerusalem will ever see lasting peace. Even now, tensions are high between Israel and the PLO over construction in East Jerusalem, which the Palestinians claim as their own.

It's all a battle over land and who will possess it.

2. **Earthquakes and Lightning.**

> Nation will rise against nation... There will be famines and earthquakes in various places.
> Matthew 24:7 (NIV)

In speaking of signals of His approaching Return, Jesus mentioned earthquakes throughout the earth. These events would be similar to birth pains of a pregnant woman, getting stronger and stronger as the end approaches. After reading on May 12, 1997 about the Iranian earthquake, I began to look into this phenomenon.

Has seismic activity increased?

The results I found were startling. The following statistics were obtained from the U.S. Geological Survey in Colorado. From 1890 (when the seismographic activity began to be recorded) to 1950, there were no more than four "killer" quakes per decade of 6.0 or greater on the Richter scale. There was an average of 2.3 earthquakes per decade. However, after the rebirth of Israel in 1948, seismic activity has changed.

Decade	6.0 or greater Quakes
1950 to 1960	9
1960 to 1970	13
1970 to 1979	51
1980 to 1989	86
1990 to 1994	over 100

According to statistics compiled from the Earthquake Data Base System of the U. S. Geological Survey, the rate of large earthquakes is escalating to unprecedented levels within the last two years. In 1996, there were seventy-two earthquakes of a magnitude of 6.5 or greater that caused injuries, fatalities or substantial damage. Through May of 1997, there have been forty-two earthquakes meeting this same standard.

To say seismic activity isn't increasing would deny the truth. As Jerry Lee Lewis once sang, "I ain't fakin'. There's a whole lot of shakin' goin' on."

3. **Bad Moon Rising.**

I will show wonders in the heavens...

Joel 2:30 (NIV)

The Hale Bopp comet blazed a path through the skies of our planet during March and April of 1996, visible to the naked eye of any casual observer. Comets have long been thought of as a sign of coming destruction. Josepheus, a Jewish-Roman historian, described a comet hovering "like a sword" over Jerusalem shortly before the city's eventual destruction in 70 A.D.

Comets seem to have the effect of inspiring terror. The suicide deaths of thirty-nine Heaven's Gate cult members, led by their leader Marshall Applewhite, punctuated this point in a sinister way. The largest mass suicide in U.S. history. As described in Elizabeth Gleich's Time magazine article of April 7, 1997, it was a perfect time for this act:

> ...with Holy Week, the vernal equinox and a partial lunar eclipse converging, all heated up by the extraordinary Hale-Bopp comet lighting the night skies. For those who go in for cosmological conjugations, it was a perfect week for an apocalypse.

These cosmic wonders are not limited to Hale-Bopp. On July 16, 1994, a fragment of the Shoemaker-Levy Comet slammed into Jupiter. The first impact alone was more powerful than the combined nuclear arsenals of our world. Through July 22, 1994, a total of twenty-one fragments hit Jupiter with a total force estimated at over 100 million megatons of TNT. They left a hole in the "king" planet half the size of earth.

The date of July 16, 1994, is incredibly significant for two reasons. First, it overlapped with the ninth of Av on the Jewish calendar. This is a date that has historically meant destruction and tragedy for Jews. Solomon's Temple was destroyed by the Babylonians of the ninth of Av, 587 B.C. Later, Herod's Temple was destroyed by the Romans on the ninth of Av, 70 A.D. Second, July 16, 1994, was also the forty-ninth anniversary of the first atomic explosion on earth at Alamogordo, New Mexico.

Comets, Jupiter, what else?

The Bad Moon Risin'. As I have mentioned before, two full lunar eclipses occurred in 1996, with the moon turning "red" on each occasion. These dates were also significant Jewish religious dates. April 3, 1996 was the Feast of Passover, and September 26, 1996 was the eve of the Feast of Tabernacles. The Hale-Bopp Comet reached its brightness peak on March 23, 1997, the same day as a third "red" moon appeared. March 23 was also Palm Sunday and the Jewish Feast of Purim. The Heaven's Gate cult took their lives on or near this same day.

It reminds me of the lyrics we use to say:

I see the Bad Moon risin'
I see trouble on the way
I see earthquakes and lightnin'
I see bad times today.

Don't go 'round tonight
Well, it's bound to take your life
There's a bad moon on the rise.

4. Melody, Miracle, and Dolly

> This is a requirement of the law that the LORD has commanded: Tell the Israelites to bring you a red heifer without defect or blemish and that has never been under a yoke.
>
> Numbers 19:2 (NIV)

In September of 1996, a strange thing happened in a small kibbutz at Kfar Hassidim in Israel. A cow was born. Her name was Melody. A red heifer without spot or blemish. The animal's birth is being hailed by Orthodox Jews as a sign from God to rebuild the Third Temple of Jerusalem, and a sign of the coming of the Messiah.

What's so unusual about a red cow?

It is believed to the first pure red heifer born in Israel in almost 2,000 years since the destruction of Jerusalem in 70 A.D. Melody was born to a black and white mother by artificial insemination with a Swiss bull. The red heifer is a rare breed indeed. According to Jewish tradition, only nine were ever recorded to have existed since the time of Moses, and the strain was long assumed to be extinct. Its ashes are necessary for a Jewish purification rite, a prerequisite for entry into the Holy Temple.

"It is written that it is the 10th heifer that the Messiah will discover and here we have the 10th heifer. This is a clear sign that Messiah is near," Rabbi Ido Weber Ellrich of Jerusalem said in an interview on Israel Radio.

Melody has been making headlines around the world, including a CNN story, articles in the *Boston Globe*, London's *Sunday Telegraph*, and *The Jerusalem Post*. The Holy Cow. She has also been referred to in more derogatory terms as a "walking atomic bomb" by the liberal press in Israel.

All of the fuss concerns the rebuilding of the Temple. Currently, perched atop the Temple Mount is one of Islam's most holy shrines, the Dome of the Rock. The Muslims aren't looking to move. Palestinian leader Yasser Arafat recently warned that the current battle over a Jewish housing project in East Jerusalem is considered by him to be the Jews' first step leading to a new Temple. On September 26, 1996, when Israel opened a new exit to a tunnel near the Mount, Muslins rioted. Politically, Israel has attempted to diffuse the situation at the Temple Mount by long ago forbidding Jewish prayer on it, and rabbis have ruled that religious Jews may not even walk on it in an impure state so as to not pollute the holiest site on the earth.

But that's what the red cow is all about—purification. However, Melody must turn three years old before she can be sacrificed and her ashes turned into a purification paste. And she must remain unblemished during the time. At her birth, Melody had a few white hairs in her tail but was considered by Jewish religious leaders as a "kosher" cow.

"We have been waiting 2,000 years for a sign from God, and now he has provided us with a red heifer," said Yehudah Etzion, the infamous leader of the 1985 plot to blow up the Dome of the Rock.

If the "miracle cow" isn't enough, you don't have to look far to yet another natural "wonder". In August of 1994, the birth of a white buffalo in Janesville, Wisconsin generated as much excitement in the Native American community as the red heifer has in Jewish circles. Bison experts estimate the odds of one being born at 1 in 6 billion.

The mythical white buffalo—a symbol of hope, rebirth and unity of the Great Plain Tribes.

The female calf's name is Miracle, and she was born on the farm of Dave and Valeree Heider. Thousands upon thousands of people from all around the world have made the pilgrimage to the Heider farm to see her.

"The arrival of the white buffalos is like the second coming of Christ," says Floyd Hand, a Sioux medicine man. "The white buffalo will bring about purity of mind, body and spirit and unity of all nations, black, red, yellow and white."

The legend of the White Buffalo is interesting.

The Sioux were starving. Two men went out to hunt and met a beautiful young woman dressed in white, floating in the air. One of the men had evil desires for the woman. He touched her and was consumed by a cloud and turned into a pile of bones.

The woman spoke to the remaining man.

"Return to your people and tell them that I'm coming."

The holy woman brought a wrapped bundle to the Sioux, containing a sacred pipe.

"With this holy pipe, you will walk like a living prayer." She taught them the value of prayer, buffalo, women, and children.

"You are from Mother Earth," she told the women. "What you do is as great as the warriors do."

The holy woman promised to return one day. As she left, she rolled over four times, turning into a white female buffalo calf.

Despite the incredible odds of Melody and Miracle being born, perhaps the oddest creature in the animal kingdom is Dolly. A sheep. In March of 1997, headlines screamed across the world:

MAN CREATES LIFE.

Researchers at Roslin Institute in Scotland had done something extraordinary—a scientific impossibility. Iam Wilmut and his team created Dolly, a cloned sheep, from a cell in an adult Finn Dorset ewe's mammary gland. An identical twin of the source sheep.

Time magazine declared in its March 10, 1997 edition:

"Not since God took Adam's rib and fashioned a helpmate for him has anything so fantastic occurred."

The nation of Israel, red moons, red cows, comets, earthquakes, and white buffaloes. What does it all mean? Or does it mean anything at all?

As a lawyer, I know that people can twist facts to say anything. But these aren't simply isolated events. If it was just one or two things, I'd say it's mere coincidence. Yet, they're not isolated. Everything is happening at the same time. A pattern of events.

People want proof, or as Cuba Gooding, Jr. said in the movie *Jerry McGuire* --"Show me the money!"

Well, I'm trying to "show you the signs." They're right in front of your face if you'll only look. See for yourself. Don't simply take my word for it. Go to your local library.

It's there. It's factual. It's the truth.

I've always heard that knowledge isn't power. It's what you do with it. Let me ask you a question. What are you going to do with knowledge of these things?

I have a suggestion. Tell others. Share the message of Jesus Christ to a lost and dying world.

> Therefore go and make disciples of all nations, baptizing them in the name of the Father and of the Son and of the Holy Spirit, and teaching them to obey everything I have commanded you. And surely **I am with you always, to the very end of the age.**
>
> Matthew 28:19-20 (NIV) emphais added.

Chapter 18

IN THIS SIGN, CONQUER

On Sunday, August 10, 1997, I dreamed that I was at a house speaking to a small group of people, sharing with them my testimony about the dreams. In concluding, I said: "I can assure you that David Doughty wouldn't be telling you this story under normal circumstances. This isn't something I volunteered for. It's not something I wanted, but I've been blessed by what's happened."

I suddenly felt the electrified feeling. I rose upward and could see that the sky outside was overcast. As I shot into the heavens, the sun shone through a break in the cloud cover. It was bright and blurry, and appeared to have a cross shape superimposed over it. Then I was awake, filled with the same tingling sensation that was becoming more and more familiar to me.

This was the last day of our summer vacation. During the drive home from New Orleans, I pondered the last installment. Before I could get a real grasp of its meaning, I had yet another one only two days later.

On Tuesday, August 12, 1997, I dreamed that I was driving my car down Glenda Street in Rayville. I was stopped at an intersection, looking back toward the Rayville Elementary School. The sky was dark and overcast. Suddenly, several holes opened in the cloud cover, bright light shining through. These holes were not directly overhead, but at more of an angle, probably 45° from the horizon. As I watched, I was lifted into the air, the electrified sensation filling my entire body.

As I awoke from the dream, the sense of urgency was as strong as it had ever been. Instantly, questions flowed through my head.

What did this mean?

Why were the two dreams so close together in time? They had always been spaced in intervals with no apparent pattern. None had been closer than a month apart. Was time running out for us? Were the few seconds in the two-minute warning almost gone?

These questions disturbed me. So many people are living their lives with no thought of God. The sins of our generation are horrifying. Time is running out, but many don't see the writing on the wall. It's happened before. Once, King Belshazzar of ancient Babylon was having a wild orgy, drinking from the holy goblets ransacked from the Temple of Jerusalem. Suddenly, the fingers of a human hand appeared and wrote on the plaster of the wall:

MENE, MENE, TEKEL, UPHARSIN.

Daniel, the same man who had been in the lion's den, revealed to the king that God had sent the hand that wrote the inscription. The words meant that God had numbered the days of his reign and had brought it to an end. The king had been "**weighed in the balances, and found wanting.**" (Daniel 5:27, NKJV). That very night, Belshazzar, the great king of the known world, was slain, and Darius the Mede took over his kingdom.

Today, our world acts as if there are no balances, no

scales, no standard. Anything goes. If it feels good, do it. Rampant homosexuality, divorce, violence, new age occultism, sexual perversion, abortion, drug and alcohol abuse. Moral decay hovers over us like stench from the dead. Anyone who condemns these sins is an old prude, judgmental, harsh, unloving. Our new motto is "live and let live." If people aren't hurting anyone, why get upset?

The fallacy of this view is that there is a standard. God's standard. Man's varies with the wind, blown by what's popular or politically correct. But God has a balance. It is unchanging.

Our world hasn't changed much since the days of King Belshazzar. If we were weighed in God's balance now, we'd still be found wanting.

On August 31, I had yet another dream, the third one of the month. I was in a forest clearing with tall pine trees surrounding me. An invisible whirlwind was swirling in front of me, the edges discernable by leaves swirling around the outer perimeter. Suddenly, I was caught up inside the whirlwind and began to rise toward the sky. I craned my head to look above me. A white light was radiating brightness. A faint golden hue tinging the surrounding clouds that framed the light. As I rose in the air, I was filled with the electrified feeling. That feeling remained, even after I awoke.

Three dreams in one month. The ramifications numbed me. Each was different, yet each left me with the same feeling.

Urgency!

As I reflected on the dreams, the whirlwind prompted thoughts of Elijah.

> As they were walking along and talking together, suddenly a chariot of fire and horses of fire appeared and separated the two of them, and Elijah went up to heaven in a whirlwind.
>
> 2 Kings 2:11 (NIV)

The imagery of the first dream, the sun with the cross wasn't new. It reminded me of the vision of Constantine, a dream almost 1,685 years old.

On October 28, 312 A.D., the Roman empire was on the verge of civil war. Constantine's army was heavily outnumbered by the imperial forces of Maxentius. Maxentius was forced to fight with his back to the Tiber River, and the only method of retreat was across the narrow Milvian Bridge.

As Constantine was readying for battle, he had a dream or vision of an unusual sign in the heavens. He saw the sun with a cross symbol over it and heard the words, "**In this sign, conquer.**" Constantine, a lifelong pagan, converted to Christianity and had his armies paint the cross symbol on their shield. That day, his armies crushed those of Maxentius, completely changing the course of western history. After Constantine consolidated his power, he issued the Edict of Milan in 313 A.D., which allowed Christians to worship free of persecution for the first time.

The sign that Constantine conquered under is just as powerful today. The cross. We need to carry the cross as a banner into our dying world. While we may not fight a military battle like Constantine, we are in a battle nonetheless. Good versus evil. We must be warriors in Christ's army to save souls from eternal damnation. Time is running out for the battle. We must intensify our efforts and go forth with boldness like Constantine, despite being drastically outnumbered. We must paint the cross on our lives, as a demonstration to the world that we are conquering in Jesus' name.

> Proclaim this among the nations:
> Prepare for war!
> Rouse the warriors!
> Let all the fighting men draw near and attack.
> Beat your plowshares into swords
> and your pruning hooks into spears.
> Let the weakling say,
> "I am strong."
>
> Joel 3:9-10 (NIV)

Be strong. Be courageous. Be bold. Be secure in the knowledge that through Christ, we can do all things.

EPILOGUE

I hope these dreams show that God is real and that He is at work in our world today. I hope you feel the same sense of urgency that Jesus **is** coming soon, and that we need to ensure that our own hearts, as well as those of our family and friends, are right with God. We're living in exciting times.

In the final chapter of the Revelation, Jesus says three times:

"Behold, I am coming soon."

Revelation 22:7, 12, 20. (NIV)

Those words were written almost 2,000 years ago. The early Christians thought Jesus would return during their lifetime, and because of that urgency, they eventually won over the same Roman Empire that had tried to destroy them.

Urgency.

Pick up a newspaper any day and it should be obvious. Floods, tornadoes, and hurricanes. Earthquakes in Iran, Armenia, China, and Pakistan. Natural disasters are occurring at an alarming rate. Cloned sheep, red heifers, white buffaloes, you name it. If this doesn't give you a sense of urgency, what will?

In 2 Peter 3:4, Peter speaks about the last days that scoffers will say:

> "Where is the promise of His coming. For since the fathers fell asleep, all things continue as they were from the beginning of creation." (NKJV)

Two thousand years have passed. Nothing.

Peter says this in response:

> "But do not forget this one thing, dear friends: With the Lord a day is like a thousand years, and a thousand years are like a day. The Lord is not slow in keeping his promise, as some understand slowness. He is patient with you, not wanting anyone to perish, but everyone to come to repentance. But the day of the Lord will come like a thief. The heavens will disappear with a roar; the elements will be destroyed by fire, and the earth and everything in it will be laid bare."
>
> 2 Peter 3:8-10 (NIV).

We as Christians today have lost our sense of urgency. We don't expect that Jesus may come any minute. The visions have not revealed to me the appointed hour of His return, but they have shown me this truth: **We need to live each day as if He were coming any minute.** We need to take the time to speak to others about God. To live right. To be ready.

In John 14:6, Jesus said, "No one comes to the Father except through me." When approached by Nicodemus, a member of the Jewish ruling council, Jesus told him, " I tell you the truth, no one can see the kingdom of God unless he is born again." John 3:3 (NIV). Jesus explained this mystery of a spiritual rebirth and told Nicodemus that "For God so loved the world that He gave His only begotten Son, that whoever believes in Him shall not perish but have everlasting life." John 3:16 (NKJV).

If you have not experienced this spiritual rebirth through Jesus Christ, please urgently consider this free gift from God. Today is all we have: Tomorrow may never arrive.

If you want to make Jesus your Lord and Master, turn to Him in repentance, ask him for forgiveness, and request that He come into your heart:

Lord Jesus,
I acknowledge that I was born a sinner and have sinned. I repent of all my sin right now. I believe that you are God's only begotten Son, that you came to this earth as a human being, and that by your death you paid the price for my sin. I believe that God the Father raised you from the dead. Come into my heart, and I will make you Lord and Savior of my life. Help me to trust, honor, and obey you. I ask that by your Holy Spirit you will lead and guide me and teach me how to live according to Your Word.
Amen.

GOD BLESS YOU.
DAVID DOUGHTY

Notes ...

Notes ...

Please write, I would appreciate your comments, or if you have an interest in me speaking to your group you can write to me at the following address.

Cotton, Bolton, Hoychick & Doughty, L.L.P.
Law Offices
608 Madeline St.
Rayville, Louisiana 71269
(318) 728-2051